JOHNNY APPLESEED

Other titles in the **Americans—The Spirit of a Nation** *series:*

EDGAR ALLAN POE

"Deep Into That Darkness Peering"

ISBN-13: 978-0-7660-3020-6

FREDERICK DOUGLASS

"Truth Is of No Color"

ISBN-13: 978-0-7660-3025-1

HARRIET TUBMAN

"On My Underground Railroad I Never Ran My Train Off the Track"

ISBN-13: 978-0-7660-3481-5

JESSE JAMES

"I Will Never Surrender"

ISBN-13: 978-0-7660-3353-5

JIM THORPE

"There's No Such Thing as 'Can't'"

ISBN-13: 978-0-7660-3021-3

JOHN BROWN

"We Came to Free the Slaves"

ISBN-13: 978-0-7660-3355-9

AMERICANS
THE *Spirit* OF A *Nation*

JOHNNY APPLESEED

"Select Good Seeds and Plant Them in Good Ground"

Richard Worth

Enslow Publishers, Inc.
40 Industrial Road
Box 398
Berkeley Heights, NJ 07922
USA

http://www.enslow.com

Library of Congress Cataloging-in-Publication Data

Worth, Richard.
  Johnny Appleseed : "select good seeds and plant them in good ground"/
    Richard Worth.
    p. cm. — (Americans—the spirit of a nation)
    Summary: "Discusses the life of Johnny Appleseed, including his childhood in
colonial America, his moveable nursery, the real stories behind his folk legend, and
the legacy he left on American history"—Provided by publisher.
  Includes bibliographical references and index.
  ISBN-13: 978-0-7660-3352-8
  ISBN-10: 0-7660-3352-X
    1. Appleseed, Johnny, 1774–1845—Juvenile literature. 2. Appleseed, Johnny,
  1774–1845—Influence—Juvenile literature. 3. Apple growers—United States—
  Biography—Juvenile literature. 4. Nurseries (Horticulture)—United States—
  History—Juvenile literature. 5. Pioneers—Middle West—Biography—Juvenile
  literature. 6. Frontier and pioneer life—Middle West—Juvenile literature. I. Title.
  SB63.C46W67 2010
  634'.11092—dc22
  [B]
                                    2008048701

Printed in the United States of America

092009 Lake Book Manufacturing, Inc., Melrose Park, IL

10 9 8 7 6 5 4 3 2 1

To Our Readers:
We have done our best to make sure all Internet Addresses in this book were active and
appropriate when we went to press. However, the author and the publisher have no
control over and assume no liability for the material available on those Internet sites or
on other Web sites they may link to. Any comments or suggestions can be sent by e-mail
to comments@enslow.com or to the address on the back cover.

✿ Enslow Publishers, Inc., is committed to printing our books on recycled paper. The
paper in every book contains 10% to 30% post-consumer waste (PCW). The cover board
on the outside of each book contains 100% PCW. Our goal is to do our part to help young
people and the environment too!

Illustration Credits: Clipart.com, pp. 37, 59; Culver Pictures, Inc., pp. 14, 21, 22, 32;
Enslow Publishers, Inc., p. 74; Fort Wayne Historical Society, pp. 3, 6, 9, 53, 72, 95;
Courtesy of James A. Watson, pp. 90, 97; © Joe Calzarette (Wikipedia.org), p. 27; Courtesy
of Karen Clemens Warrick, p. 64; Library of Congress, pp. 16, 18, 31, 49, 55, 64, 69, 70,
83; National Guard Image Gallery, pp. 12, 17; © North Wind / North Wind Picture
Archives, pp. 25, 35, 86; © Shutterstock®, pp. 10, 40, 42, 51, 107; © Tim Kiser
(Wikipedia.org), p. 88; Time & Life Pictures / Getty Images, p. 82; © 2007 Urbana
University, The Johnny Appleseed Education Center and Museum, pp. 29, 99, 105, 112.

Cover Illustration: Enslow Publishers, Inc. (Illustration of John Chapman).

CONTENTS

Johnny Appleseed

An American Hero

In June 1812, the United States went to war with Great Britain, a conflict known as the War of 1812. In August 1813, an American Indian party allied with the British ambushed and scalped a settler near John Chapman's apple tree nursery in Mansfield, Ohio. Known as Johnny Appleseed, Chapman had planted many orchards across Pennsylvania and Ohio. Following the ambush, the alarm was spread. Mansfield residents gathered inside a blockhouse to defend themselves. But the settlers believed that they could not hold out for long against a major attack. They needed someone to travel to nearby Mount Vernon, Ohio, for help. Chapman was at Mansfield at the time. He volunteered to make the dangerous trip to Mount Vernon.

Chapman traveled under cover of darkness to avoid any Indians who might be lurking in the area.

One legend says that he ran barefoot through the forest. However, he probably covered the thirty miles to Mount Vernon on horseback. As he made the journey, Chapman warned the settlers along the way.

According to one version, he yelled: "Flee for your lives. The British and Indians are coming upon you, and destruction followeth in their footsteps."

Another version says that Chapman yelled: "The spirit of the Lord is upon me, and he hath anointed me to blow the trumpet in the wilderness, and sound an alarm in the forest; for, behold, the tribes of the heathen are round about your doors, and a devouring flame followeth after them."[1]

Chapman succeeded in leading a small militia force back to Mansfield to defend the settlers there. As it turned out, there were very few hostile Indians in the area. Nevertheless, his courageous ride from Mansfield to Mount Vernon made Chapman a local hero. Indeed, the settlers of Ohio never forgot this adventure. It added to Chapman's reputation as one of the West's leading pioneers.

The Folklore and the Reality of America

Over the next twenty years, Chapman's reputation grew. Many settlers had seen this wiry man in tattered clothes. They may have spotted him canoeing down the rushing waters of the Wabash River in western Ohio. In his canoe, he carried a boatload of tiny apple seedlings. Although he looked like an odd eccentric, this was John

During the War of 1812, John Chapman traveled to Mount Vernon to get reinforcements for the Mansfield, Ohio, residents. While on his thirty-mile journey, he warned settlers of an imminent British and American Indian attack.

Many settlers may have seen Johnny Appleseed paddling his canoe down the Wabash River in western Ohio.

Chapman. The apple seedlings came from his nursery. They were being carried to settlers who lived along the river. By this time, Chapman was known as Johnny Appleseed. He was to become a great legend of the American West.

By age sixty, he was a thin, old man. This became the enduring image of him in folklore. But Chapman had been lured west almost forty years earlier. Then he was still a very young man, like so many other pioneers. Almost from the beginning, he became a teller of tall tales. He told settlers about his many narrow escapes from Indians. Chapman said that he had floated down the Allegheny River on blocks of ice. And he explained how he survived the bite of an ornery rattlesnake.

Chapman was also seen as a saintly figure living off the land. Indeed, Chapman was a deeply religious man. He brought Christian teachings to many settlers in the West. Supposedly, Chapman gave away his trees and planted orchards for anyone who wanted them.

But the reality was far different. John Chapman owned many parcels of land in Ohio and Indiana. He sold or bartered—not gave away—most of his trees. They were sold to settlers establishing homesteads in the West.

The real John Chapman was a combination of many things. He was a western pioneer, a rugged individualist, a gifted preacher, and a successful businessman. He was a teller—as well as the subject—of tall tales. Above all, Chapman's life was essentially an American story.

Chapman and Early America

During the 1630s, English colonists began to clear farms and build settlements along the fertile Connecticut River valley. The Connecticut, the longest river in New England, flows for more than four hundred miles. It begins in New Hampshire and Vermont and empties into Long Island Sound. Among the settlements along the river was Lancaster, located in southern Massachusetts.

The town grew over the next century. And some of the residents decided that "they could govern themselves more cheaply and more conveniently" in a smaller town. They decided to establish a new community called Leominster. The residents approached the leaders of Massachusetts with a petition. "Their petition to separate was granted . . . on July 4, 1740 and Leominster history began."[1]

Nathaniel Chapman, a farmer and carpenter, lived in the town of Leominster. His ancestors had arrived in Boston in 1639. Eventually, they moved southwest to the Connecticut River valley. Nathaniel Chapman married Elizabeth Simons in 1770. The Simons family had lived in Massachusetts since 1635, even longer than the Chapmans. Elizabeth's father, James Simons, was among the earliest settlers of Leominster.

After the Chapmans married, Elizabeth Chapman gave birth to a daughter. She was named Elizabeth after her mother. Nathaniel Chapman could not afford to purchase his own land. Instead, he rented a small house and farmland from Jonathan Johnson, who was married to Elizabeth's cousin. While the couple lived on this property, their second child, John Chapman, was born in 1774. John was the sixth generation of Chapmans to live in North America.

The American Revolution

Boston, only a short distance northwest of Leominster, was the center of growing unrest among the colonists. They were unhappy with many laws passed by the

An early English settlement in New England. John Chapman's ancestors arrived in Boston in 1639 and settled in the Connecticut River valley.

English parliament in London. Political leaders, such as Samuel Adams and John Hancock, protested a series of taxes levied on the colonies by Parliament. They pointed out that the colonies had no representatives in Parliament. Therefore, it was unfair for them to be taxed without any representation.

Nathaniel Chapman had joined the Leominster militia. Eventually, battles broke out between British troops stationed in the colonies and American militiamen. In April 1775, colonial and English troops skirmished in Lexington and Concord, Massachusetts. Chapman's militia company traveled along the road to Concord. But it arrived too late to participate in the small battle there on April 19, 1775. Afterward, the British troops retreated toward Boston. Colonial militiamen positioned themselves behind stonewalls and trees on the route. With their muskets, they shot many English soldiers along the way.

Once the British reached Boston, they were besieged by colonial troops. Chapman and the rest of the Leominster militia raced to the city to join the siege. In June 1775, colonial troops led by General William Prescott occupied a position on Breed's Hill. Located on the Charlestown peninsula in Boston Harbor, the hilltop overlooked the city. Prescott had learned that the British planned to occupy this position, and he wanted to stop them.

During the summer night, colonial soldiers dug up the ground on top of the hill. They built a small earthen fort. Chapman may have participated in building the fort. Or he may have helped extend the fortifications

Boston became the center of rebellious activity during the American Revolution. This is a view of Boston harbor in the eighteenth century.

from the fort along the hillside to the harbor. The next morning, June 16, the British saw what the colonists had accomplished. English warships in Boston harbor immediately began firing on Breed's Hill. In the city, British General Thomas Gage prepared to mount an attack on the colonial position.

Led by Major General William Howe, more than two thousand red-coated British soldiers climbed into small boats. Then they rowed across the harbor. Peter Brown, a colonial soldier, recalled: "There was a matter of 40 barges full of Regulars coming over to us . . . the enemy landed and fronted before us and formed themselves in an oblong square . . . and after they were well formed they advanced towards us, but they found a choakly mouthful of us."[2]

Nathaniel Chapman, John Chapman's father, joined the Leominster militia. He just missed participating in the battle at Concord, a victory for the colonial militia.

Major General William Howe led the British redcoats into battle at Breed's Hill.

As the British redcoats drew closer, colonial muskets held their fire. It was the first time that men like Nathaniel Chapman had been in battle. At Breed's Hill, they faced the world's finest army. In front of them, they could see the glint of bayonets as the British advanced. Prescott gave the famous order: "Don't fire until you see the whites of their eyes." The colonial troops waited until the British were in front of them. Then they released a loud musket volley. English soldiers were hit by the bullets and fell. White musket smoke covered the battlefield, and General Howe ordered a retreat.

The British lines reformed and advanced once again to the sound of drumbeats. They climbed up the grassy hill on that hot, June day. The muskets sounded again from behind the American defenses. Musket balls hit more and more English soldiers. Once again, they retreated, and Howe ordered his lines to reform. As the redcoats advanced a third time, the colonial militia ran out of ammunition.

This time, Howe's troops succeeded in driving the colonials back from their positions. Chapman and other members of the Leominster militia were fortunate to escape from the battlefield. As many as six hundred colonial troops were killed or wounded in the battle. The British lost more than one thousand men.

Prescott gave the famous order: "Don't fire until you see the whites of their eyes."

The British army eventually left Boston. In 1776, the war shifted to New York, where Chapman served under the command of General George Washington. While her husband was away at war, Elizabeth Chapman, back in Massachusetts, suffered from poor health. Pregnant with her third child, she had heard little from Nathaniel and did not know if he was alive or dead. Finally, a letter arrived, and she replied:

Benjamin Thompson

The American Revolution divided many families. Some joined the American army. Others, called loyalists, supported Great Britain. The Chapman family too found itself divided by the war. Nathaniel Chapman joined the colonial militia. But one of Elizabeth Chapman's cousins, Benjamin Thompson, joined the British.

Born in Woburn, Massachusetts, in 1753, Thompson later attended science classes at Harvard College. He also worked for a merchant in Salem, Massachusetts. At nineteen, Thompson became a teacher in Concord, Massachusetts. There, he married wealthy Sarah Rolf. Through her family's influence, Benjamin Thompson later became a major in the colonial militia. But he was opposed to independence and became a loyalist. In 1774, a court charged him with "being unfriendly to the cause of liberty."[3]

Thompson traveled to Boston where he joined the British army under General Thomas Gage. In 1776, he boarded a ship for Great Britain, never returning to the United States. All the while, Thompson had been experimenting with improvements in gunpowder. During the 1780s, he went to Bavaria. There, he reorganized and improved the Bavarian army. As a reward for his service, the Elector of Bavaria made him Count Rumford.

Rumford had also been conducting experiments on the nature of heat. His experiments led him to propose improved designs for stoves and chimneys. In fact, the Rumford fireplace became widely used across Europe and the United States. Count Rumford died in 1814.

After retreating twice, British lines reformed and forced the colonial army back during the Battle of Bunker Hill (Breed's Hill). This was the first time Nathaniel Chapman participated in a battle.

These lines come with my affectionate regards to you hoping they will find you in health, tho I still continue in a very weak and low condition. I am no better than I was when you left me but rather worse, and I should be very glad if you could come and see me for I want to see you. Our children are both well thro the Divine goodness. . . . I have received but two letters from you since you went away . . . and I rejoice to hear that you are well and I pray you may thus continue and in God's due time be returned in safety.[4]

Shortly after writing this letter, Elizabeth Chapman gave birth to a son. Less than a month later, however, she died. Soon afterward, the baby, named Nathaniel after his father, died too. Historians are uncertain who cared for John and his sister after the death of their mother. Because their father did not return from the army right away, they probably went to live with their grandparents. The Simons family lived nearby in Leominster.

Captain Nathaniel Chapman remained in the American army until 1780. Meanwhile, he had married Lucy Cooley from Longmeadow, Massachusetts. At thirty-four, Chapman was fourteen years older than his new wife. The couple set up their home in Long-meadow. John and his sister joined them. They lived in a small house, where Lucy Chapman eventually gave birth to ten children. One of those children was named Nathaniel, too.

Little of John Chapman's life during this period is known. According to Joe Besecker, co-director of the Johnny Appleseed Society at Urbana University, in Urbana, Ohio, "it's likely part [of his early life] was spent tending fruit trees on neighboring farms, giving him an early skill that was to serve him well in his life adventures."[5]

Nathaniel Chapman served in the American army until 1780.

An Important Decision

By the time John had reached the age of ten, America had won its independence. In 1783, the United States signed the Treaty of Paris, ending the war with Great Britain. As a result of the treaty, the United States received a large amount of British-owned lands in the West. Known as the Northwest Territories, they lay between the Ohio and Mississippi rivers. Some American Indian tribes, such as the Delaware, Ottowa, and Shawnee, lived in this area. They refused to give up their hunting grounds to American settlers. These tribes received encouragement and military supplies from the British, who still controlled Canada.

By the time John had reached the age of ten, America had won its independence.

The Northwest Ordinance of 1787, passed by the U.S. Congress, recognized the rights of the tribes to remain. But this ordinance also encouraged American settlers to move westward. Small battles broke out between American Indians and the new settlers. These led to bloodshed and death on both sides. In 1794, an American army under the command of General Anthony Wayne defeated the tribes. At the Battle of Fallen Timbers, along the Maumee River in Ohio, Wayne defeated an army of fifteen hundred warriors. A year later, the tribes signed the Treaty of Greenville. As a result of the treaty, the Indians agreed to open up a large part of the current state of Ohio to settlers.

The availability of land in the West was luring many settlers from the East Coast. Not only was the Northwest opening up, but vast lands were also available farther south in Kentucky. Daniel Boone had pioneered this area during the 1770s.

The West beckoned as settlements along the East Coast became overcrowded. John Chapman reached adulthood in the 1790s. And he was aware of the unique opportunities that lay outside Longmeadow. In the late 1780s, some Massachusetts farmers had already headed westward. They established a new settlement in Marietta, Ohio. At age twenty-three, Chapman finally decided that it was time for him to leave Longmeadow. His destination was western Pennsylvania, a frontier area. He may have heard that cheap land was available there to anyone who wanted to farm it.

Still, Chapman was venturing into new territory. He did not know what to expect. Nor was he sure how to make a living. It might have been much easier to remain in Longmeadow. But Chapman wanted to set out on his own.

The Spirit of Individualism

A heavy snowstorm blew across the Allegheny Mountains in northwestern Pennsylvania. Sheets of snow lashed the bare branches of giant oak and maple trees. Snow weighed down the delicate branches of the giant pines. Two young men trudged through the storm. They were hoping to find shelter before the storm grew any worse. One of them was lanky, dark-eyed, twenty-three-year-old John Chapman. The other was eight years younger—Chapman's half brother, Nathaniel.

"Apparently he and his younger half-brother Nathaniel worked their way westward by helping farmers with harvesting and other chores," according to Marji Hazen of the Ashland County Chapter of the Ohio Genealogical Society. Like many families from Massachusetts, they may have traveled "across northern Connecticut, south along the Housatonic River; west . . . across the Hudson by ferry . . . then by post-road across northwest New Jersey." Finally, they went west into Pennsylvania.[1]

The two Chapmans were heading toward Warren, Pennsylvania. This was a new settlement, located near Brokenstraw Creek. The Holland Land Company had purchased a large piece of property in the area. In the winter of 1797–1798, when John and Nathaniel Chapman arrived, the company had built a storehouse in Warren. An Irish immigrant named Daniel McQuay occupied the storehouse. He was an employee of the Holland Land Company.

When spring arrived in 1798, the prairie grass began to sprout around Warren. As historian Robert Price wrote, the area was "covered every summer with tall prairie grass that broke and fell over in the autumn to suggest the Indian name Cushanadauga or Brokenstraw."[2] John Chapman had come to Brokenstraw Creek with a plan to start an apple tree nursery. He reasoned that many new settlers would be coming into western Pennsylvania or going to Ohio. He knew they would want to plant apple trees.

There were several reasons Chapman believed that there would be a demand for these trees. In 1788, the

The Allegheny Mountains in Pennsylvania. John Chapman and his half brother Nathaniel crossed these mountains during the winter of 1797 before arriving in Warren, Pennsylvania.

Ohio Company was established in Marietta, Ohio. General Rufus Putnam, a hero of the American Revolution, led this company. After the war, the United States government had sold Putnam and his company 1.5 million acres in Ohio.

The Ohio Company offered one hundred acres of land to each new settler. In return, each settler had to promise to plant fifty apple trees and twenty peach trees. They had only three years to plant these trees. Along the frontier, apple orchards were an important symbol. They showed that a piece of land had been occupied and claimed by a farmer and his family. According to author Jeff Meyer, "apple trees offered the difference between successfully staking a claim and losing [the] land due to a lack of subsistence foods. Apple trees, you see, are one of the few trees that will bear usable fruit within five years of being planted."[3]

After the apples were harvested in the fall, the settlers ate some of them. But apples also had many other uses, according to Meyer. "There were baking apples, drying apples, cider apples, and dessert apples."[4] Farmers took some of their apples to cider mills in Pennsylvania. The apples were chopped between two spiked rollers that were rotated in the mill. Then the chopped apples were put in a cylinder and pressed by a rod. The juice from the apples then ran out into a container.

> Along the frontier, apple orchards were an important symbol.

Some of the juice became cider. If the cider fermented, it turned into hard cider. This was an alcoholic beverage consumed by people throughout the United States. Some of the juice was turned into apple vinegar. Farmers used the vinegar as a preservative to pickle vegetables that might spoil before they ate them. The settlers also used apples to make apple butter. This was produced by cooking the apples with cider for a long period until the concentrated mixture turned thick and soft. It was called butter because the settlers used it to spread on bread.

Apple Orchards

After arriving at Warren, Chapman spent part of the winter traveling to cider mills around Pittsburgh. A large

Americans used cider presses to make apple cider. John James used this cider press to process apples from trees planted by Johnny Appleseed in Champaign County.

town, Pittsburgh, Pennsylvania, was located where the Allegheny, Ohio, and Monongahela rivers came together. In the 1750s, the French claimed the Ohio River valley as part of their North American territories. In 1754, they built Fort Duquesne on the site where Pittsburgh currently stands. During the French and Indian War between France and England, the British captured Fort Duquesne. They renamed it Pittsburgh, after English Prime Minister William Pitt.

By 1797, Pittsburgh had a population of about fifteen hundred people. Since Chapman did not like large towns, he probably never lived in Pittsburgh. But he stopped at cider mills in the area to collect apple seeds. These were discarded after the apples had been pressed. Each apple has five pockets, called carpels. Each carpel contains seeds. Chapman probably gathered thousands of free seeds in bags that winter. A bushel basket, according to author Charles Elliot, holds three hundred thousand seeds.[5]

Chapman then returned to the area around Warren. He found fertile land along the Brokenstraw River. This was the spot he selected for his first nursery. Chapman cleared the area and planted his seeds. Although this was the beginning of Chapman's first nursery, it was not the only one in the United States. Ebenezer Zane had started a nursery in 1790 on an island in the Ohio River. Jacob Nessley had begun another nursery in Virginia. A third nursery had sprung up in Marietta in 1796. In fact, there were hundreds of nurseries by this time in the United States.

Each of these nurseries was designed to supply small apple seedlings to settlers heading west. Then settlers could begin their own apple orchards. A similar approach had been used by the first English colonists who came to North America in the early seventeenth century. As author Tim Hensley wrote, "when the first colonists arrived at Jamestown, Virginia, in 1607, there were no cultivated fruit trees in America—save for a few scattered Indian plantings—only wild crab apples, cherries, plums and persimmons. Taking a bite into a persimmon,

This is a painting of the interior of a cider mill. Chapman frequently stopped at cider mills while in Warren to collect apple seeds.

Captain John Smith [a leader of the Jamestown colony in Virginia] commented, could 'draw a man's mouth awry.'"[6] Smith meant that the persimmon tasted sour. Later, groups of colonists brought with them fruit seeds and seedlings from England. As a result, a large variety of apple and other fruit trees gradually began to grow in the English colonies.

At his home, Monticello, in Virginia, Thomas Jefferson grew a variety of fruit trees in a six-acre orchard. Many other settlers did the same thing. According to Hensley, "These so-called field or farm orchards averaged about 200 apple and peach trees each, bearing fruit for cider and [peach] brandy making, or for use as food for livestock."[7]

Colonists working at the first settlement in Jamestown, Virginia. When the first British colonists arrived in America, there were no cultivated fruit trees.

Some settlers probably brought fruit seeds and cuttings with them on their journey west. But others did not and had to buy from local nurseries. This was the role that John Chapman was hoping to fill. "When the expected settlers arrived, [he] could sell them a couple of fruit-producing trees and the seeds generated by those trees so the settlers could sow their own orchards," wrote Jeff Meyer.[8] He sold each tree for a "fippenny bit," about five or six cents.

By 1798, Chapman had established another orchard in Franklin, Pennsylvania. Franklin is located on French Creek. It flows into the Allegheny River, southwest of Warren. The French had also claimed this area during the 1750s. They built Fort Machault in the area and hoped to launch an attack on Pittsburgh. But, as the British defeated the French in 1759, the French burned Fort Machault. The British later erected Fort Venango there, but an American army captured it during the Revolutionary War. The town of Franklin, named after Benjamin Franklin, was established on French Creek in 1795.

When Chapman arrived in Franklin, there were only a few families living there. Merchants Edward Hale and George Power sold supplies to settlers who planned to establish farms. Many others bought supplies and then headed farther west. In the area around Franklin, there were about 160 men. Some had arrived with their families, but more than sixty were single.

One of these was John Chapman. Like many other people on the frontier, Chapman created a new life in the wilderness. None of these people knew what to expect. Neither did they know whether they would succeed or fail. Frankly, it might have been much safer to remain in the established settlements along the East Coast. But they were willing to risk living in unsettled land. Perhaps it was the opportunity to try something different, like planting an apple tree nursery. Perhaps it was a spirit of individualism—a sense that they did not fit into the communities in the East. As Robert Price wrote, John Chapman "was also free . . . and seemingly unwilling to be tied this early in life to any sort of conventional community pattern."[9]

Like many other people on the frontier, Chapman created a new life in the wilderness.

American Indians also hunted in the area. The Treaty of Greenville several years earlier had helped bring peace to this part of Pennsylvania. But American Indians and white settlers still fought each other. Chapman probably met Seneca Indians who came to trade at Franklin. He probably talked to others as he established an apple tree nursery along French Creek.

Chapman, who people considered very handy with an ax, cleared a space along the river. Then he planted seeds he had gathered from the cider mills. Sometimes, according to author Frank McAllister, he would plant "as many as sixteen bushels of seeds to the acre. He would stay as long as his stock of seed held out, and then would disappear as unceremoniously as he had come, only to return after a few weeks or months with another load."[10]

Johnny Appleseed is shown planting apple trees in this hand-colored woodcut. He would plant many nurseries throughout Pennsylvania. After planting the trees, he would return in a few years to prune them.

As the trees grew over the next few years, Chapman came back and pruned them. This helped them grow strong. He also built makeshift fences from twigs and fallen limbs. The fences kept out the deer that liked to eat the seedlings. Then, after they had grown, he sold the seedlings to the settlers passing along French Creek.

The Folklore Begins

During the early days in western Pennsylvania, John Chapman began to spin tall tales about himself. Tall tales generally feature a main character that seems larger than life. This character possesses abilities that are far greater than ordinary humans. These tales became popular along the American frontier. Settlers took enormous risks when they headed westward. They had experiences that were new to them and often very frightening. Floods or storms might wipe out their farms and kill their families.

As Chapman planted his nurseries, he met many settlers coming through Pennsylvania. He often told them stories about himself. One settler recalled that he had met Chapman when he was a child at the beginning of the nineteenth century. "He was a singular character," the man said. He "was very fond of children and would talk to me a great deal, telling me of the hardships he had endured, of his adventures, and hair breadth escapes by flood and field."[11]

According to one story, Chapman had run short of food during a harsh winter. He spent the cold months in a makeshift hut on an island in French Creek, eating

Paul Bunyan

There were many tall tales or legends about frontier heroes. Some of the characters were mythical, like Paul Bunyan. He was a favorite hero of American lumberjacks. Lots of wood was needed to build new towns. Lumberjacks provided the wood for the lumber business that grew up around places like Warren in the early nineteenth century. According to legend, Bunyan was born in Maine. Even as a child, he was enormous and very powerful. He grew up in the woods where he could cut down trees much faster than other men did. Eventually, he met a large blue ox named Babe. Together, Paul Bunyan and Babe cleared forests along the frontier.

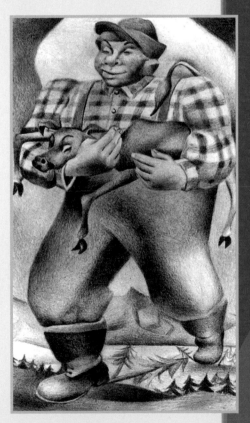

Paul Bunyan holding Babe the blue ox.

only nuts. Other stories that Chapman told described how he floated down French Creek during the winter on a block of ice. He also recalled meeting Indians that he thought may have been hostile. In one incident, Chapman said that he had escaped by walking into a lake. There, he submerged most of his body. Then he fell asleep. By the time he awoke, the Indians had gone. Chapman also bragged about his wood-chopping abilities. Indeed, he was later compared to the legendary Paul Bunyan.

> Other stories that Chapman told described how he floated down French Creek during the winter on a block of ice.

These tall tales that Chapman and others told described people who had conquered the wilderness with their extraordinary abilities. These characters served as role models for the settlers. Chapman became one of these role models. Soon the stories of his life circulated among the settlers. Gradually, he became a larger-than-life hero along the frontier.

John Henry

Unlike Paul Bunyan, John Henry was actually a real person—much like John Chapman. According to a newspaper, the *Morgantown* [West Virginia] *Dominion-Post*, Henry was a freed slave. He came to West Virginia in 1870 to work on the railroad. Soon afterward he may have defeated another railroad worker in a contest to drive steel pikes into rock. This made Henry "the [railroad] camp's undisputed steel-driving champion."[12] With an enormous hammer, steel-drivers drove holes into rock. Dynamite charges were then placed in the holes to blast out the rock. This opened up a route for tunnels through the mountains where railroad track was laid.

John Henry was a hero to railroad workers. Much of the work they did, like steel driving, was very dangerous. In fact, some of them were killed. Gradually, tall tales were told about John Henry. One claimed that he could drive holes with huge hammers in both hands. Folk songs were also sung about him. According to National Public Radio, "'John Henry' is the single most well known and often recorded American folk song."[13] One version of the song includes this stanza:

> When John Henry was a little boy,
> He was sitting on his papa's knee;
> He was looking down on a piece of steel
> Says, "A steel-driving man I will be. Lord, Lord
> A steel-driving man I will be."[14]

4

The Moveable Nursery

round 1800, John Chapman paddled his canoe south from Pennsylvania along the Ohio River. At twenty-six, Chapman was thin, with long black hair and a beard. What may have been most striking about him were his clothes. He had little money to buy anything new. Instead, he often wore old clothing that he had bartered from a local settler for some apple trees. Stories later were told that he wore an old coffee sack with holes cut in it for his arms and legs. But at least one observer who knew Chapman said that he had never seen him wear such a sack. Instead, he wore an old shirt, pants, and a long robe.

Rosella Rice, who knew Chapman when she was a child, said that "Once upon a time in exchange for trees he received an old coat. . . . It was sky blue, light and fine, firm and soft . . . with bright, silvery looking buttons on it, two rows of them, each as large as a silver dollar. His pantaloons were old and scant and short, held up with some sort of a substitute for suspenders."[1]

On his head, he might wear an animal-skin hat. Some people even told stories that Chapman sometimes wore a tin pot on his head. This was the same pan in which he also cooked his food. But historians have found no evidence to support this tale.[2]

Chapman's shoes were unusual. Sometimes he might wear sandals on his feet. But most observers agree that Chapman often went barefoot. Even in the middle of winter he walked through the snow without any shoes. As Rosella Rice wrote, "He never wore a coat except in the winter time; his feet were knobby, horny and frequently bare."[3]

> **Even in the middle of winter he walked through the snow without any shoes.**

According to one story, a settler met Chapman walking barefoot in the winter and gave him a pair of shoes. Later he ran into Chapman, walking barefoot once again. Asking what had happened to the shoes, the settler learned that Chapman had given them to another man. He seemed to need them more than Chapman did. He was always known as

John Chapman did not just plant one nursery in Pennsylvania. He wanted to provide seedlings to as many settlers as possible. His orchards sprouted up all over the western frontier.

a man who gave away food or clothing to others who seemed less fortunate.

As Chapman headed along the Ohio River, he started new nurseries. He was not content to operate from a single site in Pennsylvania. Chapman wanted to provide seedlings to as many settlers as possible. He realized that as settlers moved west, his nurseries must move with them, in places that would be most convenient to new settlements. Otherwise, he would not continue to sell his seedlings. And they could not be used to start orchards in new settlements farther west.

Apple orchards already existed in Ohio. Indeed, the French settlers had introduced them a century earlier. American Indian villages also had orchards. "But where Johnny differed" from the earlier people who had planted trees, according to historian Edward Hoagland,

> *was that he alone had set himself the task of anticipating the patterns of settlement. . . . He moved along . . . with or a step ahead of the first flying parties of settlers, to have apple trees of transplantable age ready for them when they got their land cleared. Apple vinegar was the basic preservative for pickling vegetables such as beans, cucumbers, and beats; apple butter was a principal pleasure of winter meals; and apple brandy was one of the first cash exports that could be floated downriver to New Orleans [a major city at the base of the Mississippi River]. So he began to be recognized as something of a public servant as he went about.*[4]

Chapman and Grafting

Most apple tree growers, like Jacob Nessley, practiced a method called grafting. They cut an opening in the branch of one tree, known as the stock. Then they inserted a thin wedge from the branch of another apple tree, called the scion. The scion was a tree that produced apples of superior quality. Then the two were bound together. Eventually, the stock would produce apples like those on the superior scion. Through grafting, men like Nessley could grow better apple trees. According to author Tim Hensley, "A tree grown from an apple core [seed] . . . usually bears fruit of only passable or inferior quality."[5] Grafting improves the fruit and the hardiness of the apple trees. One well-known nurseryman who practiced grafting was Henderson Lewelling. He created a fruit nursery in Iowa in the 1830s.

Chapman, however, did not believe in grafting. He thought that it was wrong to kill or wound any living thing, plant, or animal. Grafting involved cutting a piece from a living tree. "The correct method," he supposedly said, "is to select good seeds and plant them in good ground and God only can improve the apples."[6]

Around 1800, Chapman established a nursery at Carrollton in the Ohio Territory. The following year, he began other nurseries at Wellsburg in present-day West Virginia and possibly at Brilliant across the river. This brought him near the nursery already established by Jacob Nessley.

New Nurseries

From the Ohio River, Chapman headed north along the Muskingum River. The Muskingum runs for about one hundred miles. It was a natural route for settlers to follow into the Northwest Territory. At the mouth of the Muskingum, where it joins the Ohio River, the town of Marietta had been established. Marietta had been named after the French Queen Marie Antoinette. The settlers who founded Marietta wanted to thank France for helping the United States during the American Revolution. Chapman passed Marietta. But there were already orchards there. So he traveled farther north.

His route took him up the Muskingum River toward Zane's Trace. Chapman probably planted orchards along the trace. This was one of the routes that settlers would use. He then headed up the Licking River. A few families had already begun to establish farms along this forty-mile river. The Licking ran into the Muskingum, which flowed into the Ohio River. Along this watercourse, farmers could ship their crops to market at Marietta and Pittsburgh.

In 1801, Chapman may have planted an orchard on the farm of Isaac Stradden along the Licking River. This

Zane's Trace

Zane's Trace, or road, had been built by Ebenezer Zane. He was a nurseryman and a hero of the American Revolution. Born in 1747 in Virginia, Zane had later married Elizabeth McColloch. Together, the couple had thirteen children. In 1769, Ebenezer Zane and his brothers built Fort Henry at present-day Wheeling, West Virginia. They successfully defended the fort from several American Indian attacks during the American Revolution.

During the 1790s, Zane and his brothers received permission from Congress to build a road from Wheeling that passed through southern Ohio to Maysville on the border with Kentucky. As payment for the work, Congress gave the Zanes parcels of land along the road. Zane intended to sell the land to settlers heading west. According to the Federal Highway Administration, "In the early stages, Zane's Trace was wide enough for only a horse and rider but not a wagon. Many of the pioneers used the rivers for transportation, so Zane built ferries at each of the river crossings. After having built a ferry at the mouth of the Licking River, a small town developed, eventually named Zanesville."

Beginning in 1803, the trace was widened so wagons could pass along the road. "Settlements sprang up along the way," according to the Federal Highway Administration, "with businesses such as taverns and inns that catered to the travelers. Farmers used the road to transport their crops to market."[7]

nursery may have provided some of the trees that were later transplanted by settlers into their own orchards. Chapman returned to the area repeatedly over the next five years. He traveled along the Licking and Mohican rivers as well as north along Owl Creek. When there were only one or two families in the area, Chapman planted apple seeds. He usually planted on fertile soil along a river. Chapman then enclosed the nurseries with brush to keep out the animals.

Then he might stay in the area for awhile, lying in a hammock. "Or he might strip slabs of bark from a giant elm," wrote Edward Hoagland, "and lay them against it for a lean-to, or toss together a quick Indian hut of poles and bark, stretching out on a bed of leaves inside."[8] Soon afterward, Chapman moved on, returning after the trees had grown. He probably pruned the trees to keep them as healthy as possible.

Mount Vernon

By 1805, enough settlers had entered the area to establish the town of Mount Vernon, located on Owl Creek. Mount Vernon was named after the home of George Washington on the Potomac River in Virginia. The town included 240 lots for settlers. They were laid out in a grid, with seven streets running horizontally and three streets running vertically. Outside the town were apple orchards and peach orchards. At least as early as 1806, James Loveridge bought some of Chapman's Owl Creek trees to create an apple orchard.

Over the next few years, Mount Vernon grew. The settlers cut trees and built log cabins. Ben Butler, one of the settlers, converted his cabin into a tavern. Farms were carved out and cornfields were planted. Some of the harvest was used for food and feed for farm animals. But some of it was also converted into corn whiskey and sold at Butler's tavern.

Expanding the Nurseries

In 1806, John Chapman traveled down the Ohio River from Pennsylvania. He paddled one canoe, with another lashed to it. The canoes carried leather bags of apple seeds destined for Owl Creek and the Mohican River. The canoes, according to historian Edward Hoagland, were "daubed with mud and draped with moss to keep the load moist."[9] Chapman's journey took him past Marietta, Ohio. His father Nathaniel and stepmother Lucy had moved their family there from Longmeadow in 1805. They established a farm on Duck Creek, a few miles north of Marietta. Chapman's father died two years later. But his stepmother continued to run the farm with several of her children.

From Marietta, Chapman headed north. Along the Muskingum River, near present-day Coshocton, a group of settlers were already laying out farms. Chapman established a small orchard in the area. It later provided apple trees for the farmers' orchards. These settlers included the families of Martin Cox, John Ely, Timothy Hawkins, as well as David and Thomas John.

Many settlers built log cabins in the growing town of Mount Vernon. Chapman provided apple trees to all those who needed them from his nearby orchard on Owl Creek.

On the Mohican River, Chapman planted his seeds, creating another orchard. This was located near present-day Tiverton, Ohio. The orchard stretched for about one acre. It was started with about three bushels of apple seeds.[10] The seedlings that grew there provided trees for settlers, such as Isaac Draper, and many others who moved into the area. According to author Frank McAllister, "Many of the trees he disposed of to farmers for transplanting and in some cases he would sell an entire orchard on the spot he had originally chosen. If the customer was poor, as most pioneers were, he could have the trees for nothing, or Johnny would take any old piece of clothing in exchange." If a pioneer could afford to pay, the price was a "'fippenny-bit,' and immediate payment was never required."[11]

> "If the customer was poor, as most pioneers were, he could have the trees for nothing . . ."

By 1809, Chapman's nurseries were growing along the Muskingum River. Among the settlers in the area was William Stanbury. According to author Ophia D. Smith, "At Stanbury's house, John often spent the night, usually sleeping out in a grove near the house. Stanbury said that Johnny ate only vegetables. Some of Johnny's friends have said that he was very fond of milk and honey, because he considered them heavenly foods."[12] Chapman did not eat meat. That would have meant killing an animal. He did not believe in killing any living creature.

Chapman and Animals

The pioneers in Ohio regularly told stories about John Chapman's love of animals. When they could no longer carry heavy loads, settlers often abandoned the horses. Time and again, Chapman rescued these horses, which he passed during his trips along the trails. "Every autumn," according to Frank McAllister, "he would start out in a diligent search of the woods and clearings of such strays or cast-offs, that he might care for them till they died of old age."[13] With some of the money he made from selling trees, Chapman paid farmers to feed and care for these horses. Some he took with him to carry his heavy bags of apple seeds.

At the same time, legends arose about Chapman's treatment of other animals. According to one story, he was clearing a spot for a new orchard. Suddenly, a rattlesnake bit him. Chapman reacted immediately. He hit the snake with the scythe that he had been using to cut the grass. After being treated by a doctor, Chapman was fearful that he had badly hurt the snake. Unfortunately, his blow had killed it. "Poor fellow," he reportedly said later, "he only just touched me, when I in the heat of my ungodly passion put the heel of my

Legends grew about Chapman's treatment of animals. He even felt sorry for killing a rattlesnake that had bit him.

scythe upon him, and went away. Some time afterward I went back and there lay the poor dead fellow."[14]

Another story involved a yellow jacket. It flew into Chapman's clothing and began to sting him. Instead of killing the insect, he removed it without harm. Chapman did not believe in killing an animal that simply reacted according to instinct. One evening, mosquitoes flew into a fire that he had kindled to cook his meal. According to legend, Chapman put out the fire to save the insects.

On another cold evening, he built a fire at the end of a hollow log. Then he realized that a bear and its cubs were sleeping inside. So Chapman put out the fire. He preferred to sleep in the cold rather than deprive the bears of their home. Chapman often told this story. But no one knew whether it was true. If so, he may have also saved himself from a very angry mother bear trying to protect her cubs.

Johnny Appleseed

As the settlers established their farms, John Chapman was a constant visitor. For example, he did not build a cabin in Mount Vernon. Instead, he stayed at the homes of Benjamin Butler and other settlers. He might spend a night or two sleeping on the floor in front of the fire. Then Chapman moved on to other settlements, established new nurseries, and stayed with other pioneers. He was widely known across Ohio because of his apple orchards. Settlers relied on him for their apple trees, and he was welcomed into their homes.

As settlers established their farms in Mount Vernon, Chapman constantly visited and stayed in the homes of different settlers. Throughout his life, he rarely had a home of his own. Chapman is at right, seated on the floor, reading a book.

Gradually, they began to refer to him, not as John Chapman, but as Johnny Appleseed.

In 1809, he had finally gathered together enough money to purchase two lots in Mount Vernon. Chapman paid the owner, Joseph Walker, fifty dollars for them. They were located near his apple nursery. One lay along Owl Creek, while the other was north of the creek. This was the first land that Johnny Appleseed had ever owned. Until that time, he had simply selected a location and planted his orchards. Since there were few people around to claim the land or settle it, the apple trees grew undisturbed. No one cared for them while Chapman traveled. Once he returned to the orchard, he pruned the trees and sold them.

Chapman had plenty of trees to sell. In one short note, he wrote: "October 12, 1812. For value received I promise to pay or cause to be paid to Benjamin Burrel one hundred and fifty trees at my nursery . . . in the month of March such as they are when called for. John Chapman."[15] He had put down roots in Ohio. His nurseries were prospering and he was supplying the nearby settlers with apple trees.

But, over the next few years, his life in Ohio would undergo tremendous change.

The War of 1812

A s settlers poured into Ohio, they encountered American Indians still living in the area. These included the Delaware, Shawnee, and Wyandot people. There was an Indian village at Greentown along the Mohican River and another Indian settlement at Jerometown. Johnny Appleseed had warm, friendly relations with most of the American Indians living in the area. According to author Rosella Rice, "The Indians all like him. They regarded him from his habits as a man above his fellows. He could endure pain like an Indian

Warrior; could thrust pins into his flesh without tremor. Indeed so insensible was he to acute pain that his treatment of a wound or sore was to sear it with a hot iron and then treat it as a burn."[1] They also knew that he endured snakebites and withstood multiple bee stings.

At the time, many settlers on the frontier used herbal medicines and folk remedies to cure illnesses. Johnny Appleseed was no different and had a great knowledge of many herbs. According to author Frank McAllister:

> *Johnny planted seeds of many medicinal herbs in the woods through which he traveled. Doctors were few and far between in the wilderness, and Johnny wished to make up for this lack as far as he could. By his efforts hundreds of miles of forests were carpeted with fennel, catnip, horehound, pennyroyal, rattlesnake root, and other [herbs] that our ancestors used in sickness.*[2]

Apparently his favorite herb was mayweed. It grows about two feet high and is sometimes referred to as "Johnnyweed." According to pioneer stories, Chapman believed that it was a natural medicine. He believed that mayweed could prevent malaria if mixed with tea. This serious disease was carried by mosquitoes and killed many settlers.

Chapman often carried seeds and cuttings of medicinal plants—herbs—with him. And he gave these to the settlers he visited. He also taught them how to use these medicinal herbs.

Hopocan

The Delaware living at Jerometown were led by a chief named Konieschquanoheel, meaning "maker of light." The Delaware nicknamed him Hopocan, which means "tobacco pipe." The white settlers called him Captain Pipe.

Hopocan was born about 1725, somewhere in Pennsylvania. During the American Revolution, Hopocan did not want to support either the British or the Continental Army. According to the Ohio Historical Society, his mother, brother, and some of his children were killed by American soldiers in 1778. Nevertheless, Hopocan continued to remain neutral. But later that year, the Americans demanded that Hopocan and the Delaware join in an attack on the British at Fort Detroit. Hopocan continued to remain neutral. So the Americans destroyed a Delaware village at Coshocton in 1781. This persuaded Hopocan to join the British.[3]

After the American Revolution ended, Hopocan and some of his people moved to Ohio. In 1788, they were living along the Ohio River when settlers arrived in Marietta. Hopocan led his warriors on raids against the pioneers settling in the area. Six years later, Hopocan and his followers recognized that the white settlers could not be defeated. He signed treaties giving some of his land to them. But the treaties were frequently violated.

Eventually, Hopocan moved to Jerometown. As the War of 1812 approached, he left Jerometown and moved his followers to Canada. Historians are not certain when he died. Hopocan may have died as early as 1794. Or Hopocan may have lived until sometime around 1812–1814.[4]

American Indians were thought to regard Chapman almost like a medicine man. Medicine men (and women) were eccentric—different from the rest of the tribe. They possessed enormous power from the spirit world. This gave them the ability to heal sick people. Their herbs and potions, the Indians believed, could cure illness. Like the medicine men, Chapman was eccentric and he possessed the power of a healer. This was another reason why American Indians and white settlers alike often welcomed Chapman.

Tecumseh

Tensions grew between white settlers and American Indians along the Ohio frontier. Indians who wanted to keep the settlers out were led by the Shawnee chief Tecumseh and his brother Tenskwatawa, known as the Prophet. Born around 1768 in Ohio, Tecumseh, like his oldest brother Chiksika, had become a much-feared warrior. In 1791, he helped defeat the American army sent into the Northwest Territory. But three years later, at Fallen Timbers, he found himself on the losing side in the battle against General Anthony Wayne. Many American Indians had opposed the Treaty of Greenville, signed in 1795. One of them was Tecumseh. He believed that the Indians had no right to sign the treaty. Tecumseh argued that they had given away land that they did not own.

Tecumseh also opposed the Treaty of Fort Wayne signed in 1809. William Henry Harrison, the governor of the Indiana Territory, negotiated this treaty. Under the terms of the treaty, a group of Indian delegates gave up 3 million acres of land to the United States for settlement. But none of the Indians lived on these lands. And Tecumseh claimed that they had no right to sell them.

Tecumseh

Tecumseh began traveling among the tribes in the South and Northwest. He tried to bind them together in a large confederacy. Meanwhile, his brother, the Prophet, inspired many Indians with his spiritual visions. The Prophet said that a vision had enabled him to predict a solar eclipse in 1806.

In 1808, Tecumseh and the Prophet established a village along the Tippecanoe River in Indiana. There, they tried to gather together Indians from many tribes in an alliance to force out white settlers. In 1811, Tecumseh traveled south to gather more supporters. General Harrison marched toward Tippecanoe. With an army of more than one thousand soldiers, he hoped to frighten the Prophet and his warriors.

At dawn on November 7, 1811, the Indians attacked Harrison's camp. The American soldiers were awakened by the sounds of musket fire and Indian warriors. Nevertheless, Harrison's men formed a defensive position and stopped the attack. After a two-hour fight, the Indians retreated and abandoned their village at

Tippecanoe. General Harrison later burned the village to the ground.

Causes of the War of 1812

About seven months after the Battle of Tippencanoe, the United States declared war on Great Britain. The War of 1812, as it was called, had a variety of causes. One of them was the conflict in the West. The British in Canada supported Indian leaders like Tecumseh. They wanted him to create a strong American Indian confederacy. Great Britain hoped that Tecumseh could hold back the westward movement of American settlers. This would provide protection for British territory in Canada and along the Great Lakes.

The United States, on the other hand, saw Canada as a threat to America's future. Great Britain's trade with Canada increased. At the same time, the British placed heavy taxes on American exports. These were being sent to English colonies in the West Indies. This meant that American merchants could not compete with the Canadians. Many Americans also felt that it was the destiny of the United States to take control of Canada. Congressman John Harper put it this way: "The Author of Nature [God] marked our limits in the south, by the Gulf of Mexico . . . and on the north, by the regions of eternal frost [northern Canada]."[5]

American leaders also believed that they could easily conquer Canada. As an article reflecting the view of U.S. President James Madison said, Canada was "in the power of the U. States because it consists of a long and slender chain of settlers unable to succor or protect each other."[6] Indeed, the Canadian population was only about 500,000 compared to 7.5 million people living in the United States.

In addition, there were few British troops in Canada. Most of them were fighting in Europe against France. Emperor Napoleon Bonaparte directed the French armies.

The War in the West

As the War of 1812 began, the United States launched an invasion of Canada. General William Hull directed this invasion. Hull's army of about two thousand soldiers marched across the Detroit River into Canada in July 1812.

Hull moved slowly north from Fort Detroit. He failed to attack a British fort at nearby Amherstburg. Hull felt that his army was too weak to be successful. Meanwhile, British General Isaac Brock made a successful attack west of Hull's force. The British captured the American post at Mackinac Island on Lake Huron. According to historian Carl Benn, this victory "inspired a good portion of the natives of the upper lakes to take up arms against the United States."[7]

The victory also persuaded Hull to retreat. He left Canada and withdrew his army to Fort Detroit. While Hull sat at Detroit, Indian tribes wiped out an American force at Brownstown on August 5. They had been bringing supplies to Hull. So Hull sent a force of six hundred men south to open up his supply lines.

But they were ambushed on August 9. Less than a week later, General Brock and his army of 1,300 British soldiers and Indian warriors appeared in front of Detroit. Brock immediately called on Hull to surrender. "It is far from my intention to join in a war of extermination," Brock wrote, "but you must be aware that the numerous body of Indians who have attached themselves to my troops will be beyond control the moment the contest commences."[8]

At first, Hull refused to surrender the fort. Then British cannon began to bombard Detroit on the evening of August 15. The next day, Hull decided to give up the fort. He feared what the American Indians might do to his troops if they were defeated. Although his forces outnumbered Brock's, Hull surrendered his army on August 16, 1812.

Chapman and the War of 1812

The loss of Detroit frightened the settlers along the western frontier. By 1812, pioneers had pushed north from the Mohican River toward Lake Erie. Cabins had already been built along the Huron River, as settlers established new farms there. Among them was Caleb Palmer, a surveyor. He had purchased land in the area about 1810. His farm was located in the Firelands section along the Huron River. John Chapman lived part of the year with the Palmer family. He may have also planted an apple tree nursery nearby.

Chapman also had a nursery growing farther south at the town of Mansfield, Ohio. Samuel Martin was the first pioneer to build a cabin at Mansfield in 1808. As historian A. J. Baughman wrote, the first settlers had to clear the land and remove the trees. Then they laid out streets and a town square. Although the trees were easily cut, removing stumps was more difficult.

"As there was no public fund for the removal of the stumps," Baughman added, "an ordinance was passed that men convicted of a misdemeanor be sentenced to 'dig out a stump.' . . . The most frequent offence was intoxication, and sometimes when a pioneer wanted to take a [drinking] spree, he would first dig up a stump—thus paying in advance."[9]

Later, settlers at Mansfield built a blockhouse to defend the community. In case of attack by American Indians, settlers could retreat inside the blockhouse. From there, they could fire their muskets at the attackers. They might hold them off until reinforcements arrived. After the loss of Detroit, settlers at Mansfield feared that an American Indian attack could happen very quickly.

John Chapman had always maintained friendly relations with the Indians. He could travel through their villages very easily. He even attended their council meetings and knew their plans. Therefore, Chapman was asked to serve as a scout for communities in the region. His job was to travel along the Huron River and warn the towns if he saw an Indian and Canadian war party approaching. On August 21, Chapman apparently thought that he had spotted a war party. Chapman ran through the woods toward the settlements. "Flee for your lives—the Canadians and Indians are landing at

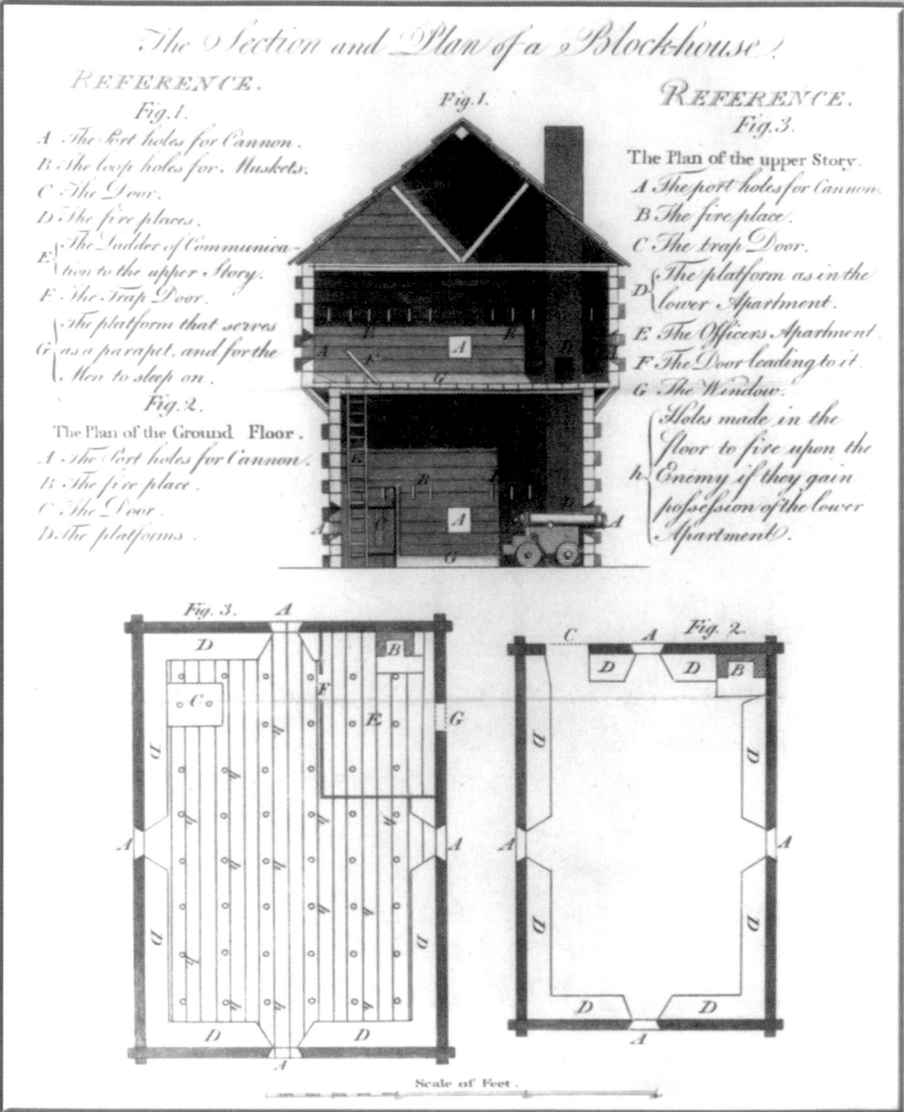

The Section and Plan of a Block-house.

REFERENCE.

Fig.1.

A. The Port holes for Cannon.
B. The loop holes for Muskets.
C. The Door.
D. The fire places.
E. The Ladder of Communication to the upper Story.
F. The Trap Door.
G. The platform that serves as a parapet, and for the Men to sleep on.

Fig.2.

The Plan of the Ground Floor.

A. The Port holes for Cannon.
B. The fire place.
C. The Door.
D. The platforms.

Fig.1.

REFERENCE.

Fig.3.

The Plan of the upper Story.

A. The port holes for Cannon.
B. The fire place.
C. The trap Door.
D. The platform as in the lower Apartment.
E. The Officers Apartment.
F. The Door leading to it.
G. The Window.
h. Holes made in the floor to fire upon the Enemy if they gain possession of the lower Apartment.

Fig.3.   Fig.2.

Scale of Feet.

This is a section and plan of a blockhouse (above). Settlers built blockhouses to protect themselves against American Indian attacks. At right, a reconstructed blockhouse in Mansfield, Ohio, is shown.

Huron," he yelled.[10] One settler named Hanson Read remembered Chapman's warning. He immediately gathered his family together, and they hid their valuable possessions in the woods. Then the Reads headed toward Mansfield.

Most of the settlers gathered around Caleb Palmer's house. They decided to leave the Firelands area and head south for Mansfield. With Palmer leading them, the settlers hoped that they might not be seen by the Indian and Canadian war party. As they headed south, the settlers received more news. A messenger joined them in the woods. He said that a large party of British troops and Indians—nine hundred in total—were marching through Ohio.

Chapman's warning that the enemy was coming turned out to be a "false alarm."

As it turned out, there was no invading force—it was simply a rumor. Instead, there were nine boats of American prisoners who had been released by the British at Detroit. Indeed, Chapman's warning that the enemy was coming turned out to be a "false alarm," according to historian Robert Price.[11]

However, the mere threat of an Indian invasion prompted the settlers to take action. By this time, Captain Pipe had left Jerometown to live in Canada. But the Indian settlement at Greentown remained. Militiamen led by Colonel Samuel Kratzner marched to Greentown. His mission was to persuade the American Indians there to leave and relocate in Urbana.

However, Kratzner was unsuccessful in persuading the Indians to leave. He called on help from the Reverend James Copus. He was a friend of the Indians who had lived in the area for several years. Copus convinced the Greentown Indians to leave their homes. He persuaded them to move to Urbana, saying that their village would be safe. Later, after the war had ended he said, they could return to Greentown. The Indians did not want to abandon their homes. But they agreed to go temporarily. Soon after they left, some of Kratzner's soldiers returned to Greentown and burned the village. As the American Indians were marching away, they turned around and saw smoke rising from their village. On the way to Urbana, they stopped in Mansfield. There, the American Indians were kept under close guard.

Deaths on the Frontier

The Greentown residents were upset and angry over the loss of their village. Word of the treatment of these American Indians spread across northern Ohio. American Indian attacks occurred along the frontier. The local militia began to erect blockhouses in the area of Jerometown. Meanwhile, settlers were killed along the Mohican River. On September 10, 1812, Frederick Zimmer and his family were attacked at their cabin near Greentown by a band of five Indians. With the Zimmers was a neighbor named Martin Ruffner. They had moved into the area around 1803. A man named Philip living in the house was sent to get help. According to the Ashland County Historical Society, "Ruffner fought bravely,

The Death of Toby

The daughter of an American Indian named Toby visited Greentown when the villagers were removed and held at Mansfield. Toby went to Mansfield to get his daughter and take her to another reservation. But he was not permitted to do so by Kratzner's soldiers. Refusing to leave his daughter in Mansfield, Toby snuck into the town and took her away. Two soldiers followed him and finally caught up with Toby about two miles out of town. They shot him, but Toby escaped. He managed to crawl to a nearby creek. It was later named Toby's Run. The two soldiers returned with reinforcements and searched for Toby. After finding him, one of them killed him with a blow from a tomahawk. His daughter escaped and spread the tale of Toby's death among other American Indians. This may have helped convince many of them to carry out massacres against the settlers.

to the extent that when he ran out of ammunition, he used his rifle like a club. He was eventually killed, and scalped, and then the attack proceeded to the rest of the family. Kate Zimmer was the last killed."[12]

The Zimmers were not the last people to lose their lives along the frontier in 1812. The Reverend Copus and some militiamen went to the Zimmer home after the massacre. Philip led them back there, too late to save the Zimmers. After seeing what had happened, Copus and his family left the area to stay at a block-house at Beam's Mill, near Mansfield, where some militiamen were stationed. After staying there several days, Copus and his family decided to return to their cabin. Local militia leaders advised them not to return. But Copus did not listen to their advice.

On September 15, while the militiamen were washing at a spring, they were attacked by at least forty-five Indians. Some of the militia retreated to Copus's cabin, where the battle continued for about five hours. Copus was killed along with several militiamen. Then the Indians left the area. Soon after, reinforcements arrived to rescue the rest of Copus's family. Some of them were still alive inside the cabin.

The Frontier War

During 1813, the war along the frontier continued. In August, a settler named Levi Jones was ambushed and scalped by an American Indian war party. Jones lived near Johnny Appleseed's nursery at Mansfield. Jones's death spread panic among Mansfield residents. While

Naval battles on the Great Lakes became important during the War of 1812. American naval forces won a decisive victory over the British on Lake Erie in September 1813.

they gathered in a blockhouse, Chapman went on his famous ride to Mount Vernon for reinforcements.

Meanwhile, U.S. forces launched new attacks on Canada. These occurred along Lake Ontario, Lake Erie, and the Niagara River. In September, American naval forces on Lake Erie won a decisive victory against the British. By taking control of Lake Erie, the Americans cut off the British at Fort Detroit from the rest of Canada. As a result, they abandoned Detroit and retreated to the east. Tecumseh and his Indian allies accompanied the British soldiers. At the Battle of the Thames River on October 5, 1813, American forces defeated the British. Tecumseh was killed while leading his Indians during the bloody battle.

According to author Carl Benn, with the death of Tecumseh, the "native dream of an independent

Tecumseh was killed during the Battle of Thames River on October 5, 1813.

homeland effectively ended. In the weeks that followed, the majority of aboriginal survivors either went home and made peace with the Americans or limped east to seek shelter behind the British lines."[13]

The war continued for more than a year. However, there was little conflict along the Ohio frontier. The War of 1812 officially ended in 1814 with the Treaty of Ghent, but neither side gained any new territory. Meanwhile, Johnny Appleseed had gone back to planting his nurseries.

Tecumseh was killed while leading his Indians during the bloody battle.

Business and Religion

B y 1814, John Chapman had planted his apple orchards across a large part of central Ohio. His nurseries had sprouted along the Muskingum River, Owl Creek, the Licking River, and branches of the Mohican River. Orchards had also been planted around Mansfield and Mount Vernon and along the Huron River heading north to Lake Erie. Hundreds of settlers had bartered for his trees or purchased them. But "immediate payment was never required," according to Frank McAllister.

"Johnny usually took a note from the customer, and of such promises-to-pay he collected a . . . number during his career, but it is not on record that he ever tried to collect any of them."[1] Indeed, any settler who could not afford to pay for apple trees generally received them for free.

Until then, Chapman had followed the same routine. He selected a fertile piece of land. Frequently it was located near a river. This was not only a place where settlers traveled and would see the nursery. But it was also a fertile location where the trees were likely to flourish. Except for the lots in Mount Vernon, Chapman did not own any of the land. All of it had belonged to someone else. It was owned by a land company, a town, or an individual settler. Or it was simply wilderness that belonged to no one.

On May 31, 1814, Chapman signed a ninety-nine-year lease for a piece of property near Mansfield. Mrs. Jane Cunningham also signed the lease. She was apparently a friend of Chapman's as well as an early resident of Mansfield. Together, they leased 160 acres of land. This was known as a quarter section. Such a long-term lease—the use of the property in return for rent—was almost the same as an outright purchase. The property had been set aside in the Mansfield district for school buildings. But until they were built, the land could also be leased to individuals. The cost of the lease was an annual rent of $19.20. To hold onto the 160 acres, Chapman had to put up a cabin on it. He also had to develop three acres of the property. The new property would become the site of another apple orchard.

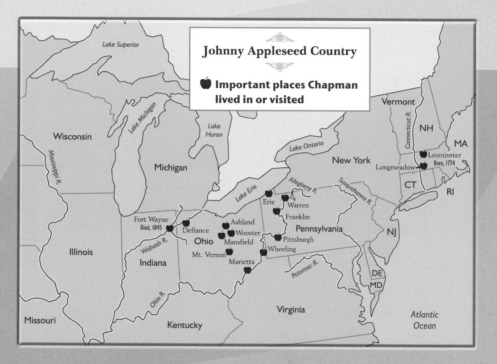

Johnny Appleseed planted nurseries throughout the present-day states of Pennsylvania, Ohio, and Indiana. This map shows some of the important places in John Chapman's life.

This was only the first piece of property that Chapman acquired after the War of 1812. Later in the year he bought another piece of property near Mansfield. Early in 1815, he purchased property near the village of Wooster, Ohio, for $100. And later that year, Chapman signed another contract for property. This was located on the Black Fork of the Mohican River. It lay near the Indian village of Greentown. Each piece of property was a quarter section.

Chapman had apparently saved enough money from the sale of apple trees to make the land purchases. After all, his lifestyle was extremely simple. His clothes were castoffs, given to him by friends. His food consisted of nuts and fruits, gathered from the wild, or vegetables, such as corn and potatoes. These were often given to him by the settlers or the local Indians. Perhaps he even bartered for some of his food with apple trees.

Johnny Appleseed did not believe in putting his money in a bank.

Chapman's home also cost little or no money to build. On the property that Chapman purchased, he built a hut. It was constructed from planks of wood cut from trees in the forest. Sometimes, he hid his extra cash in the house. Apparently, Johnny Appleseed did not believe in putting his money in a bank. But he did have a strong belief in the United States. In 1816, for example, he delivered the Fourth of July speech at a town along the Huron River. There were few forms of entertainment along the frontier. So settlers gathered together on a holiday like Independence Day. They sat outside on a warm summer day, enjoyed a picnic, and listened to a speech by a local speaker.

A Successful Landowner

In 1818, Chapman continued his land purchases. He bought two more pieces of property around Mansfield. One of these was located in town. The other lay outside where Chapman planted a nursery. Around 1820, some of the residents came out to purchase apple trees. They saw Chapman living under several large pieces of elm bark, which formed a lean-to. He offered them a simple meal of cornmeal mush.[2]

Among his favorite dishes, according to author Edward Hoagland, was "journey bread." It was made "by boiling green corn till it was half done, drying it again in the sun, then browning it in hot ashes when ready to eat, pounding it fine, and possibly stirring in birch or maple syrup or summer berries or honey."[3]

Local settlers sometimes helped Johnny Appleseed build a cabin. In 1819, for example, Cornelius Vandorn and his brother gave Chapman a hand with his house. Author Ophia Smith wrote:

> After sitting down and talking for awhile . . .
> Johnny poked in the ashes with a stick and pulled
> out some roasted potatoes. From under the log he
> pulled a bag of salt. This simple fare he offered his
> guests, saying, 'This is the way I live in the
> wilderness.' He went on to say, 'I could not enjoy
> myself better anywhere. I can lie on my back, look

up at the stars, and it seems almost as though I can see the angels praising God, for he has made all things for good.' One of the boys opened their sack of provisions and laid out . . . bread and butter and dried venison, inviting Johnny to share it. Johnny ate some of their bread and butter.[4]

Each time, he purchased a new piece of property, Chapman made it a point to visit the nearby settlers. This was his way of letting them know that he had apple trees to sell. Often he would bring them small gifts, such as a piece of colorful cloth or ribbons for the children. Or he might give them herbs, such as catnip or Johnnyweed. He might also bring the settlers small amounts of tea. He purchased the tea with extra money from the sale of his trees.

Chapman often spent the night with the settlers. As Rosella Rice recalled, "I remember distinctly of falling over one of Johnny's well filled sacks [of apple seeds] early one morning immediately after rising. It was not light in the room at the head of the stairs, and it was not there when I went to bed the night before. It seems that he arrived at night, and for safe keeping the sack was put upstairs, while he lay beside the kitchen fire."[5]

Chapman usually shared a meal with the settlers he was visiting and then sat in front of the fire to tell stories. One settler recalled that

Johnny partook of a hearty supper, and gave us a full history of the Seymour [Zimmer] family and blockhouse scenes, etc. When bedtime arrived, Johnny was invited to turn in, a bed being prepared

for his especial accommodation, but Johnny declined the proffered kindness, saying he chose to lay on the hearth by the fire, as he did not expect to sleep in a bed in the next world, so he would not in this.[6]

According to other accounts, Chapman also told stories about his adventures in the woods. They included his encounters with rattlesnakes, wasps, bears, and mosquitoes. Through these tales, he helped create the legend of Johnny Appleseed. The legend also tried to explain why Chapman was a bachelor. Stories went around that he had been jilted by a young woman in Massachusetts. Afterward, he had never found another woman to love and remained single for the rest of his life.

Chapman always demonstrated a great fondness for children. When he visited a settler's home, children immediately were drawn to him. They often sat in his lap and listened to his stories. Chapman especially loved his half sister Persis's children. She had moved to Marietta a decade earlier with her father. By 1816, Persis and her husband, William Broom, had moved to a farm in Perrysville, on the Black Fork of the Mohican River. Chapman spent part of each year visiting there.

Chapman—The Missionary

As he visited settlers along the frontier, Chapman not only brought the stories of his life. He also preached about Christianity. Poets Rosemary and Stephen Vincent Benét wrote:

Of Jonathan Chapman
Two things are known,
That he loved apples,
That he walked Alone . . . .

The Stalking Indian,
The beast in its lair
Did no hurt
While he was there.

For they could tell,
As wild things can,
That Jonathan Chapman
Was God's own man.[7]

During the early nineteenth century, the United States was gripped by a powerful religious revival known as the Second Great Awakening. John Chapman played an important role in the Second Great Awakening. At some point in his life, he had developed a strong belief in God. This may account for much of his generosity. He often shared what little he had with others.

After he arrived in a settler's home and had dinner, Chapman usually took out his worn Bible. As his friends sat around the fire, Chapman asked, "Will you have some fresh news right from Heaven?"[8] Then he began to read from the Bible. In addition, Johnny Appleseed carried the writings of an eighteenth-century Swedish religious leader, Emanuel Swedenborg.

Indeed, as author John Stockwell wrote, "One cannot understand John Chapman . . . unless one understands his religion." Chapman followed four rules that Swedenborg had developed for his religion. The first

The Great Awakenings

The First Great Awakening occurred in the American colonies during the 1730s. This attempt to increase religious devotion and strengthen beliefs had begun in England and continued in North America. Preachers warned their parishioners that they would be damned in Hell unless they demonstrated their love of God. Among the best-known clergymen was the English preacher George Whitefield. He made seven trips to America to preach to the colonists. Other preachers imitated his style, according to historian Christine Leigh Heyrman. With dramatic gestures, "sometimes weeping openly or thundering out threats of hellfire-and-brimstone, they turned the sermon into a gripping theatrical performance."[9]

The First Great Awakening had run its course by the middle of the eighteenth century. By the early nineteenth century, a Second Great Awakening was under way in the United States. In the western states and territories, settlers gathered together in large camp meetings in the wilderness. These were especially popular in Virginia, North Carolina, Kentucky, and Ohio. Participants sang hymns, listened to sermons from dynamic preachers, and dedicated themselves to God.

At the core of these meetings were religious conversions. People asked themselves, "What can I do to be saved?" They recognized that they had been sinful and vowed to repent of their sins. Then they surrendered themselves to God—the "moment of conversion." Sinners believed that only God could save them.[10]

was to read the Bible on a regular basis. The second rule was "To submit everything to the will of Divine Providence." The third rule was "To observe in everything a propriety of behavior and to keep the conscience clear." And the fourth rule was "To obey what is commanded, to discharge with fidelity the functions of my employment and the duties of my office, and to render myself in all things useful to society." Stockwell wrote that Chapman followed all of these principles in his life.[11]

> As his friends sat around the fire, Chapman asked, "Will you have some fresh news right from Heaven?"

Chapman was actively involved in the Church of the New Jerusalem. A letter sent from Philadelphia to Manchester, England, the headquarters of the church, mentioned Chapman. "There is in the western country a very extraordinary missionary of the New Jerusalem. A man has appeared who seems to be almost independent of corporal [physical] wants and sufferings. He goes barefooted, can sleep anywhere, in house or out of house, and live upon the coarsest and most scanty fare. He has actually thawed the ice with his bare feet."[12]

According to author Ophia Smith, "Chapman was always eager to make converts to the New Church."[13] As Chapman sat in a settler's home, he often read from Swedenborg's books. Somehow, he had developed a relationship with William Schlatter, a wealthy merchant in Philadelphia. Schlatter was a member of the local Swedenborgian Society. He published many of the

John Chapman was a very religious man and almost always had a Bible with him during his travels. This photo shows a worn Bible that once belonged to Chapman.

Emanuel Swedenborg's teachings became popular in Europe and eventually came to the United States. Swedenborgian societies took shape in Pennsylvania and Ohio.

writings of Swedenborg. Schlatter also sent the books along with his shipments of cloth to other towns in North America. In a letter written in 1817, Schlatter wrote that "I have sent some books to Mr. Chapman . . . he travels about in Ohio and has much to do with apple trees."[14]

Chapman also worked closely with a minister named Silas Ensign. The Reverend Ensign arrived in

Emanuel Swedenborg and His Beliefs

Emanuel Swedenborg was born in Stockholm, Sweden, in 1688, and later attended the University of Uppsala. His father was a theology professor at the university and a bishop. After completing college in 1709, Swedenborg went to England and other countries. There, he studied science and mathematics. Later, he came back to Sweden and published a scientific journal. He also published books on philosophy and chemistry. Swedenborg believed that all matter was made up of moving particles—a forerunner of atomic theory.

During the 1740s, Swedenborg experienced a spiritual awakening. In a vision, Jesus Christ told him to leave his scientific studies and devote himself to religious faith. Swedenborg began writing books on the Bible. He believed that individuals existed at the same time in the spiritual and physical worlds. He also wrote that God creates every living thing out of his love and wisdom. Therefore, all creatures are sacred.

After Swedenborg's death in 1772, Swedenborgian societies began to take shape in England. They were called the Church of the New Jerusalem. Gradually, societies were founded in the United States, based on Swedenborg's writings. They were located in Philadelphia, western Pennsylvania, Maryland, Virginia, and Ohio.

Mansfield and built a cabin nearby during 1818. He also became a leader of a Swedenborgian group in the area. Chapman was one of its most active members. In 1821, Chapman even offered to give some of his land to the Church of the New Jerusalem in exchange for additional books. Schlatter wrote to one of the church leaders in Manchester, "I have received a letter from a zealous member of the New Church, and one who appears most anxious to spread the doctrines of truth. He offers land for books but as our societies have no books on hand it is out of their power to supply him."[15]

Chapman wanted to leave books behind with settlers whom he visited so they could read and study them. Because he was usually short of books, however, he often took out chapters from his own copies. These were small sections, or signatures. Then he left the signatures with the settlers until he returned on another visit and collected them.

"He loved reading," wrote author Jeff Meyer, "and he loved ideas. Because of this he became a lending library. Most settlers had not been able to bring many books on their trek west, so he would gratefully take one they offered, read it, and swap it at the next stop for a book that the family had finished reading."[16]

Some settlers remembered him reading from the books. "We can hear him read now," a woman recalled, "just as he did that summer day, when we were busy quilting upstairs, and he lay near the door, his voice rising . . . and thrilling—strong and loud as the roar of wind and waves, then soft and soothing as the balmy

John Chapman was an active member of the Swedenborgian group called the Church of the New Jerusalem. Chapman is shown speaking to a preacher in Ohio.

airs that quivered the morning-glory leaves about his gray beard."[17]

Some settlers compared Chapman to St. Francis of Assisi. This thirteenth-century monk lived a simple life, dressed in tattered clothes, and befriended animals. Chapman's belief in Swedenborg's teachings also seemed to support his view of American Indians. As Swedenborg put it, "All things in the world exist from Divine Origin . . . clothed with such forms in nature as enable them to exist there and perform their use and thus correspond to higher things."[18] Indians deserved the same respect as white settlers. Both were created by God, according to Swedenborg.

Chapman developed a reputation along the frontier for his devout religious beliefs. When David Ayers was still a boy, his family lived on the Black Fork of the Mohican River. One day in 1822, they received a visit from Chapman. He left behind chapters of his Swedenborgian books for the family to read. This was only one of his stops. Many other families also received the Swedenborgian writings.

As Poet John W. Stockwell wrote:

John Chapman—"Johnny Appleseed," so named,
Caused wild sown soil and soul—to be reclaimed
From wilderness; and creeds in darkness framed.
He harmed no living thing. He served the maimed . . . .
This tree that finds its way to light above
Is man's response to God's creative love . . . .
The Christian faith of Swedenborg, far-famed,
His guide, his soul inspired, his self-hood tamed.[19]

Johnny Appleseed traveled along the Mohican River many times, planting nurseries and visiting families. The Black Fork of the Mohican River in Ashland County, Ohio, is shown.

Nevertheless, the church grew slowly in the western communities. Many settlers did not agree with its teachings. However, Chapman worked closely with the Reverend Ensign to build up his local Swedenborgian Society. Meanwhile, additional societies gradually arose. They were located in settlements along the Muskingum, Licking, and Huron rivers. The work of Johnny Appleseed may have influenced their development.

Chapman developed a reputation along the frontier for his devout religious beliefs.

As William Schlatter wrote to a Swedenborgian preacher in Virginia, "Mr. Ensign says when he first went there, there was but one receiver and that was Mr. John Chapman, whom you must have heard me speak of, they call him John Appleseed out there."[20]

Chapman Transforms the West

After the War of 1812, the town of Perrysville, Ohio, was established on the Black Fork of the Mohican River. By 1817, there were about ten houses in the small community. In the nearby woods, farmers let their cattle and hogs roam, eating whatever food they could find. "The inhabitants have enough to eat and drink," said an observer, "except cider."[1] But Johnny Appleseed was solving that problem.

Since about 1809–1810, Chapman had been planting orchards along the Black Fork. Chapman had anticipated that settlers might be arriving in the area. Soon after they appeared, he began providing them with apple trees. He sold trees, for example, to a settler named John Oliver and to another pioneer named Ebenezer Rice. In fact, Chapman became a frequent visitor to the Rice cabin.

Soon after Perrysville was founded, Chapman's half sister Persis moved there. Her husband, William Broom, often worked for Chapman in his nurseries. When Johnny Appleseed traveled to his other orchards, Broom took charge of the nurseries on the Mohican. At Chapman's request, he gave about fifty trees to a young man named David Hunter, the sole supporter of his orphaned eight brothers and sisters. Chapman knew that he needed help and generously gave him the trees. After receiving the seedlings, Hunter planted them on his farm. Eventually, he developed an orchard with hundreds of trees.[2]

> **At Chapman's request, he gave about fifty trees to a young man named David Hunter, the sole supporter of his orphaned eight brothers and sisters.**

About this same time, the United States was experiencing an economic downturn. It was known as the Panic of 1819. Many banks closed, and people lost their life savings. Farmers could no longer pay the mortgages on their land and had to give up their farms. As a result, there may have been fewer settlers to buy apple trees.

During the early 1820s, Chapman lost some of the land he had leased in the previous decade. This included the piece of property he had leased with Jane Cunningham near Mansfield in 1814.

Moving Westward

Although Chapman had lost some of his land, he did not intend to stop purchasing new property. But instead of expanding his nurseries in central Ohio, he planned to move west. In 1817, several Indian tribes in western Ohio had signed the Treaty of Maumee Rapids. Under the terms of the treaty, the Wyandot, Seneca, Delaware, Shawnee, and Potawatomi agreed to turn over 4 million acres to the United States. In return, they received small pieces of land farther west and cash payments.

After the treaty was signed, the area opened up to new settlers. But even before a large number of them arrived, Chapman was there planting apple trees. During the 1820s, he began establishing nurseries along the broad Maumee River. He also planted orchards along its tributaries, the Blanchard and Auglaize rivers. In 1828, settlers along the Blanchard River reported that Chapman was already there with trees for sale. He had also planted a nursery near the site of present-day Mount Blanchard on the Blanchard River.

In 1794, General Anthony Wayne had built Fort Defiance, located where the Maumee and Auglaize rivers flow together. This later became the bustling town of Defiance, Ohio. By 1828, Chapman had planted a nursery near Defiance. It provided apple trees for the settlers coming into the area. South of Defiance, Chapman had started another orchard near the village of Florida on the Maumee River.

Meanwhile, Johnny Appleseed had begun leasing property again. In 1828, he made an agreement with Jacob Harter to lease land on the Auglaize River south of Defiance. In return, he agreed to give Harter forty apple trees in five years. Ten miles away, he leased another piece of property for forty trees from a settler named Picket Doute. This lay on the St. Mary's River. This was followed by a third lease from William Hedges for land along the St. Mary's. In return, Chapman agreed to give Hedges one thousand trees over the next ten years.

Meanwhile, Chapman sold one piece of property he had purchased many years earlier on Owl Creek at Mount Vernon. He received thirty dollars for the town lot. Chapman's decision to sell the Mount Vernon lot may have been influenced by his changing travels. During the 1830s, Johnny Appleseed spent only part of the year in eastern Ohio. The rest of the time, he cared for his nurseries in the western part of the territory.

One settler asked him if the trees in his nurseries came from grafts. "He answered no, rather decidedly," according to historian Robert Price, "and said that the proper and natural mode was to raise fruit trees from the seed."[3]

During the spring and summer months, Chapman transported seeds from the east to his nurseries in western Ohio. In 1830, one observer saw him "seated in a section of a hollow tree which he improvised for a boat, laden with apple seed fresh from the cider presses of a more eastern part of the country, paddling up the Maumee River, and landing at Wayne's fort, at the foot of Main Street, Fort Wayne."[4]

General Wayne had founded Fort Wayne, Indiana, after the Battle of Fallen Timbers. By the time Chapman arrived, Fort Wayne was a busy trading community. There were warehouses along the river, bustling shops, and numerous taverns. Chapman brought apple seeds to the Fort Wayne area and began to establish nurseries there. One of them was located east of Fort Wayne. Others were planted on the north and south sides of the Maumee River. They were located on farms owned by Fort Wayne settlers.

During the summer of 1834, Chapman purchased a piece of property west of Fort Wayne. He bought about forty-two acres for $2.50 per acre. Clearly he had made enough money to pay cash for the land instead of apple trees. In 1836, he purchased another piece of property near Fort Wayne. This was almost nineteen acres for $1.25 per acre. Near the Ohio border, Chapman purchased another seventy-four acres for a nursery.

Over the next few years, Chapman returned to these nurseries over and over again. He came during the spring with fresh apple seeds. On the forty-two-acre plot near Fort Wayne, for example, there were eventually fifteen thousand trees. Around 1834, Persis Chapman Broom, her husband, William, and their four daughters moved from Perrysville to Indiana. There, her husband continued to help Chapman care for his nurseries. During the months when he went back to eastern Ohio,

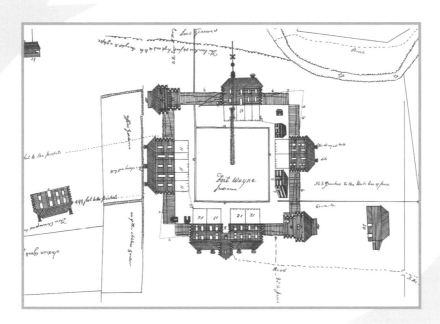

In the early 1830s, Chapman planted several nurseries in the bustling trade community of Fort Wayne, Indiana. He also purchased property there.

Chapman probably left William in charge of the apple orchards. These nurseries continued to grow. And Chapman returned to them each spring during the 1830s and 1840s. Settlers reported seeing him at his nurseries along the St. Mary's and Auglaize rivers.

Last Years

By 1840, Johnny Appleseed was about sixty-five years old. Many settlers never reached that age. So Chapman was considered to be an old man. However, his pace did not seem to slow down. He continued traveling back and forth between his orchards. Settlers who saw him during those later years described him as "an oddity called Johnny Appleseed."[5] He looked like a poor, old derelict in his tattered clothes.

Some settlers may have shied away from Chapman. But others welcomed him into their homes. His niece Lucy Jane and her husband William Johns had established a farm in Van Wert, Ohio. This was located near the Indiana border. Chapman visited his niece's family often and established a nursery nearby. In 1842, he visited his half brothers and a half sister, who were living in the Muskingum Valley.

> "Then he drew out from his bosom one of his old dingy books and read aloud to us."

"The last time we saw him," wrote Rosella Rice, "was one summer day when we were quilting. A door opened out upon the ground, he laid his little bundle on the sill, lay down on the floor, resting his head on the parcel. Then he drew out from his bosom one of his old dingy books and read aloud to us. It is a picture which will remain long with me."[6]

Chapman also spent time in the home of William Worth and his family. They lived north of Fort Wayne. He had begun visiting them in 1836 because they lived near one of his nurseries. Over the next decade, he returned again and again. In March 1845, when John Chapman was seventy-one, he was visiting the Worth family. Apparently, he received word that cattle had gotten loose inside his nursery nearby. Chapman went out on a cold, snowy night to move the cattle. He also needed to fix the fences around his orchard. Then he

This was the last surviving apple tree planted by Johnny Appleseed discovered on a farm in Ohio. Chapman continued to plant apple trees until he died in 1845.

returned to the Worth home. The Worths later said that he had been dressed in "a coffee sack, as well as the waist sections of four pairs of old pants cut off and slit so that they lapped . . . around his hips, under an antiquated pair of pantaloons."[7]

Chapman apparently developed pneumonia after that frigid night and died. After his death, an article appeared in the *Fort Wayne Sentinel*: "Died in the neighborhood of this city, on Tuesday last, Mr. John Chapman, better known as Johnny Appleseed. The deceased was well known through this region by his eccentricity, and the strange garb he usually wore. He followed the occupation of nursery-man."[8] He was buried in a graveyard a few miles from Fort Wayne.

After Chapman's death, John Harold—the husband of one of Persis Broom's daughters—made a final inventory of Chapman's estate. It included an old mare, many thousands of apple seedlings, and five pieces of property.

The Legacy of Johnny Appleseed

John Chapman was a unique character along the American frontier. He made a permanent impression on the people who met him. Even when he could no longer visit or sell apple trees, people did not forget Chapman or what he had accomplished in their communities.

Following John Chapman's death in 1845, stories began to appear about him. In 1846, author

T. S. Humerickhouse wrote an article about him for *Hovey's Magazine of Horticulture*. Humerickhouse lived in the Muskingum Valley. He described Chapman's nurseries in the valley and how he came back to tend them each fall. A year later, Henry Howe wrote *Historical Collections of Ohio*. Howe interviewed people who had known Chapman in Mansfield and other towns. He described Chapman's nurseries. Howe also retold the stories about Chapman's love of bears and rattlesnakes as well as his simple clothing.

During the 1850s, Johnny Appleseed began to appear in fictional writings. In 1858, for example, the Reverend James F. McGaw wrote a novel called *Philip Seymour, or Pioneer Life in Richland County, Ohio*. The book described the Copus Massacre, and Chapman was one of the characters in the story.

Poet and writer Rosella Rice knew Chapman when she was a child. She had grown up in Perrysville, Ohio, and he had visited her home. In 1882, she delivered a speech about Johnny Appleseed in Ashland County, Ohio. The speech was given at the dedication of a monument to the Copus Massacre. Rice's speech was later reprinted in *Godey's Lady's Book*, one of the most popular magazines of the nineteenth century. Concluding her speech, she said, "His bruised and bleeding feet now walk the gold-paved streets of the New Jerusalem [Heaven.]"[1] Rice presented a full picture of Chapman's life. She emphasized his role as a Swedenborgian preacher as well as a nurseryman.

About the same time, author Lydia Maria Child's poem about Chapman had become popular. It eventually became one of the most famous verses ever written about Johnny Appleseed.

Weary travelers, journeying west,
In the shade of his trees find pleasant rest;
And they often start, with glad surprise,
At the rosy fruit that round them lies.

And if they inquire whence came such trees
Where not a bough once swayed in the breeze,
The answer still comes, as they travel on:
"These trees were planted by Apple-Seed John."[2]

Meanwhile, an article on John Chapman also appeared in *Harper's New Monthly Magazine* in 1871. Founded in 1850, *Harper's* was one of the leading literary magazines in the United States. It featured articles written by well-known authors like Mark Twain and sketches by famous artists, such as Winslow Homer. W. D. Haley's piece, titled "Johnny Appleseed: A Pioneer Hero," was very important. Other writers based their works on the article. This "was in some ways the most influential piece ever written about Chapman," according to his biographer Robert Price. The article "lifted a localized legend out of its Middle Western locale and gave it sudden coast-to-coast prominence before a public that accepted it immediately and warm-heartedly as a national possession to be cherished."[3]

Haley began his article with Chapman's work along Licking Creek in 1801: "[He] was at the time of his appearance on Licking Creek, twenty-six years of age, and whether compelled in his eccentricities by some absolute misery of the heart which could only find relief in incessant motion, or governed by a benevolent [obsession], his whole after-life was devoted to the work of planting apple seeds in remote places." Haley described the coffee sack that Chapman wore, his bare feet, and the tin pot worn on his head. He emphasized Chapman's love of children and how American Indians admired him. Haley also retold the legends that Chapman had first told. These included the story about his gentleness toward the wasp that stung him and the mosquitoes around his campfire. Finally, Haley described Chapman's religious beliefs and the way he spread them throughout the countryside.

> The highly romantic tale told by Haley inspired many untrue folk tales later written about Chapman.

According to Haley, Chapman died in 1847—two years later than the actual date—at the home of friends in Indiana. After reading from the Bible, he went to sleep on the floor of their cabin: "[I]n the early morning he was found with his features all aglow with a supernal light, and his body so near death that" he could not speak. Soon afterward, according to Haley, Chapman died. "A laboring, self-denying benefactor of his race, homeless, solitary, and ragged, he trod the thorny earth with bare and bleeding feet, intent only upon making the wilderness fruitful."[4]

The highly romantic tale told by Haley inspired many untrue folk tales later written about Chapman. According to these, he married an American Indian woman in Missouri. He was a friend of George

Washington and Daniel Boone. He also fought in the Battle of Fallen Timbers and at the Battle of Tippecanoe.

Many poems were also written about John Chapman. Lydia Maria Child wrote about him in old age. Other poems described his warm relationships with American Indians. They recalled his travels and his love of children. Author Florence Boyce Davis provided this description of him:

> *Who comes there with a leathern sack*
> *Bulging over his homespun back,*
> *Barefoot, hatless, alert and slim—*
> *What is the mission that calls to him?*
> *His thin gray frock is thin and worn,*
> *Stretched in service and bramble-torn . . .*
> *And his eyes with gentle fervor glow*
> *Like the soft, wild eyes of the mountain doe.*[5]

One of the best-known poets to write about Chapman was Vachel Lindsay. During the early twentieth century, he published a series of books about Johnny Appleseed. According to Lindsay, "He was a New England kind of saint."[6] More recently, Johnny Appleseed has been the subject of many stories for children.

Myths and Realities

Sometimes the stories about John Chapman have greatly exaggerated what he accomplished. They may have overstated his personal qualities. Nevertheless, the facts of his life are more than enough for him to be called a very remarkable man. The real Johnny Appleseed was a rugged individualist. He was the type of man that many Americans admire. Chapman was a pioneer. He accomplished what no one before him had done. He charted a new direction that others could follow. Very few people have the courage to undertake this kind of adventure.

Around 1800, Chapman set off from Massachusetts into the wilderness. He left no letters. Therefore, historians do not know whether he had already decided what he intended to do when he reached Pennsylvania.

> **Chapman was a pioneer. He accomplished what no one before him had done.**

But he found a niche for himself. Chapman showed that he was a very shrewd entrepreneur. He collected free apple seeds and then planted them on land that he did not own. As seedlings appeared, Chapman turned around and sold them. They were bought by pioneers who wanted to plant orchards on their own land.

As poet Gertrude Martin put it:

> *From the hillside's ordered orchard trees*
> *and from the chimney stones,*
> *Where the gnarled old stump puts forth*
> *a clump of bloom to hide its bones,*
> *Each tree tells Johnny Appleseed that*
> *the trails he loved to tread*
> *Still are wild and sweet where he set his*
> *feet, long after he is dead.*[7]

Chapman recognized that his product was in great demand by the new settlers. Apple trees stood as a

Johnny Appleseed has been memorialized in books, poems, folk tales, and more. This photo shows his gravesite in Fort Wayne, Indiana.

symbol of a flourishing homestead. And, even more importantly, the apple had a variety of essential uses in early America. Settlers not only ate apples and used them in a popular spread, apple butter, they also relied on apple vinegar to preserve their food. They cooked apples into their desserts and pressed them to make apple cider.

Chapman wanted settlers to have the apple trees that they needed. In part, he was probably motivated by a desire to help other people. But he was also a smart businessman. Chapman saw an opportunity and figured out a way to fill it. In addition, he did it—at least in the early years—with little or no financial expense to himself.

Why He Stood Out

Of course, Chapman was not the only nurseryman on the frontier in the early nineteenth century. Yet most of the others have disappeared from history. Chapman, on the other hand, is remembered. Indeed, he even received a nickname, Johnny Appleseed. One reason may have been his unusual behavior. No doubt, some of the stories may have been exaggerated. But historians seem to agree that he did sleep in hollowed-out logs. And he dressed in ragged clothes. This made him stand out—he was unusual, an eccentric. Chapman obviously did not care much about his appearance or his home. A much-higher calling motivated him.

However, he did not leave his success as a nursery-man to chance. Chapman never stopped promoting

John Chapman also helped spread his folklore by spinning tales about himself. He was a celebrity who became widely admired on the western frontier. This is an aged five-cent stamp with Johnny Appleseed on the front.

himself. He told stories about his adventures in the wilderness. These rapidly became part of the folklore on the frontier. They marked him as someone who was larger than life. Chapman became a folk hero. He was a celebrity, widely admired by the pioneers in the West.

> **Chapman became a folk hero. He was a celebrity, widely admired by the pioneers in the West.**

They seemed to enjoy talking to him, hearing his stories, and sharing in his unusual life.

Life on the frontier was hard and tiring. Settler families spent long days in the fields, planting and later harvesting their crops. Then there were long hours spent cooking, washing, and spinning clothes. Settlers welcomed any diversion. And Chapman provided it. He visited new settlers when they arrived. He went to their homes, brought them small gifts, shared his stories and tall tales, and told them about his apple trees.

Chapman's success was a model for other settlers. In 1891, Chapman's fame was growing. As the *Cincinnati Commercial Gazette* wrote: "There's a hero worth the singing that no poet's lips have sung/ A prophet of the wilderness whose deeds have found no tongue."[8] If he could succeed, other settlers believed that they could, too. One way to do it was to build a thriving homestead in the wilderness. Then they had to keep it going in the face of harsh weather and the threat of American Indian attacks. This meant establishing a permanent settlement. A hallmark of these settlements was apple orchards.

But Chapman was far from a high-pressure salesman. He was known for his gentleness. He had developed a reputation as someone who kept the best interests of the settlers in mind. If they could not afford to buy his trees, then he would barter them for food or clothing. In some cases, he gave his apple seedlings away. His generosity became legendary across the frontier.

Chapman was also a very religious man. He helped spread the Swedenborgian beliefs. Money did not seem to be very important to him. Nevertheless, he still managed to acquire enough to eventually buy property in Ohio and Indiana. During his life, Chapman owned twenty-two pieces of land totaling 1,200 acres.[9] After his death, the land was sold off. Chapman seemed to have a knack for anticipating where new settlements would spring up. And that was where he bought his property, planted his trees, and established his nurseries.

While other nurserymen stayed in one place, Chapman kept moving. As poet Florence Boyce Davis wrote:

> *Day in day out, and year by year,*
> *From Licking Creek to the far frontier,*
> *Johnny Appleseed comes and goes,*
> *Comrade of every wind that blows;*
> *The hills are his and the winding streams,*
> *His bark canoe, and his cherished dreams.*[10]

Chapman knew how to predict the next good location to establish another nursery. Chapman followed the rivers, which were the main routes to new settlements. He paddled the Ohio, the Licking, the

Muskingum, the Maumee, the Blanchard and the St. Mary's rivers. By knowing where the settlers—his customers—would be, he could often get there ahead of them. This gave him time to plant his seeds. Then he raised his seedlings and sold them to the new settlers.

The Missionary

But Chapman carried more than apple seedlings. He brought with him his Christian teachings. This also made him unusual. Chapman was revered along the frontier because of his spiritual beliefs. He brought not only tales of his own life but stories from the Bible. Chapman spread the beliefs of Swedenborgianism. According to historian Edward Hoagland, "He was compared to John the Baptist, a voice in the wilderness heralding a new religion."[11] Like John the Baptist, Chapman lived a simple life, close to nature.

Chapman and Modern Times

During the twentieth century, monuments to John Chapman appeared. One of them was erected in 1940 in Leominster, Massachusetts, where he was born. A Johnny Appleseed Campground opened in Fort Wayne, Indiana. And each year, in September, the city of Fort Wayne hosts a Johnny Appleseed Festival.

In 1994, the Johnny Appleseed Heritage Center was founded in Ashland, Ohio. A drama about Chapman's life was staged there in 2004–2005. At Urbana University in Urbana, Ohio, there is also a Johnny Appleseed Education Center and Museum. According to the

Chapman and Transcendentalism

There is no historical evidence that John Chapman read the works of the Transcendentalists. However, he seemed to exemplify their teachings. The Transcendentalist Movement began in Massachusetts during the 1830s. It was led by Ralph Waldo Emerson, a poet and philosopher. Another important Transcendentalist was writer Henry David Thoreau. The Transcendentalists believed in living close to nature. They saw the natural world as the work of God. They also wrote that human beings could find spiritual truths. These would "transcend" their rational experiences. Through these spiritual truths, they could live better lives.

In the 1840s, Thoreau spent two years living in a simple cabin. This was located near Walden Pond in Concord, Massachusetts. Emerson owned the land. Later, Thoreau wrote about his experiences in *Walden*, published in 1854.

Chapman is still remembered today. The Johnny Appleseed Society at Urbana University made this gavel as a memorial to the pioneer. The gavel was made out of wood from an apple tree Johnny Appleseed had planted in Apple Creek, Ohio.

Center, it "holds the largest collection of [material] and written information about the life of John 'Appleseed' Chapman known to exist in the world." The collection includes an old cider press and bark from some of the trees that Chapman planted.

Some of these trees continued to grow during the twentieth century. In 1994, the last of Chapman's trees was identified on a farm in Ohio. The farm was 140 years old and owned by the family of Marilyn Algeo Wilkins. The tree was largely rotted away. According to Bill Jones, founder of the Johnny Appleseed Heritage Center, "We believe it was planted in the 1830s when the farm was first established, but we'll never know exactly how old it is because the interior has decayed."[12]

The giant tree was identified as a Rambo. This was a species of apple that was considered a favorite by

Johnny Appleseed. According to author Charles Elliot, it is "firm and tart and suitable for either cooking or eating."[13] Cuttings were taken from the tree before it was uprooted by a tornado. Although Chapman did not believe in graftings, the cuttings were used to grow new trees. They became the descendants of seedlings planted by Johnny Appleseed.

Facts About the Apples

Apples are one of the most popular foods in the United States. Here are some facts about them.

- 7,500 apple varieties are grown across the world.

- 2,500 apple varieties are grown in the United States.

- Only the crab apple grows naturally in North America.

- The apple tree was first grown in Europe around the Black Sea.

- The first apple tree nursery was opened in 1736 in New York.

- A species called the Newton Pippin was exported from the colonies in the 1760s.

- Currently, the Golden Delicious is the most popular apple in the United States.

CHRONOLOGY

1774—John Chapman is born in Leominster,
 Massachusetts.

1775–
1783—The American Revolution is fought in
 North America.

1780—The Chapman family moves to Longmeadow,
 Massachusetts.

1794—American Indians are defeated at the
 Battle of Fallen Timbers.

1797—John Chapman moves to Pennsylvania.

1798—Begins to plant his apple tree nurseries.

1800—Begins planting nurseries along the Ohio River.

1801—Plants orchards along the Licking River in Ohio.

1805–
1806—Plants orchards in Mount Vernon, Ohio, and also
 starts nurseries along Owl Creek and Mohican
 River; Chapman family moves to Marietta, Ohio.

1809—Johnny Appleseed purchases his first plots of land
 in Mount Vernon, Ohio; the Treaty of Fort Wayne
 is signed.

1811—American Indians defeated at Battle
 of Tippecanoe.

1812–
1815—The War of 1812 is fought in North America.

1812— Copus massacre occurs.

1813— Chapman rescues settlers at Mansfield during
an Indian attack; Levi Jones is murdered by
American Indians.

1814— Johnny Appleseed buys land near Mansfield, Ohio.

1817— The Treaty of Maumee Rapids is signed.

1818— Chapman buys additional land around Mansfield;
helps build the Swedenborgian Society in Ohio.

1819— The Panic of 1819 occurs; Chapman loses some
of his land.

1821— Offers to swap land for books to help spread
the Swedenborgian religious beliefs.

1820s—Plants orchards in western Ohio; purchases
more land.

1830— Visits Fort Wayne, Indiana; plants nurseries.

1830s—Establishes more nurseries in western Ohio
and Indiana; buys additional land.

1845— Chapman dies.

CHAPTER NOTES

CHAPTER 1
An American Hero

1. William E. Leuchtenburg, "John Chapman (Johnny Appleseed)," in Susan Ware, ed., *Forgotten Heroes* (New York: Free Press, 1998), p. 14.

CHAPTER 2
Chapman and Early America

1. *History of Leominster, Massachusetts*, n.d., <http://members.aol.com/Leominster476/History.html> (March 1, 2008).
2. "The Battle of Bunker (Breeds) Hill," *The American Revolution*, n.d., <http://www.theamericanrevolution.org/battles/bat_bhil.asp> (March 3, 2008).
3. "The Life and Legend of Count Rumford," *Rumford Historical Society*, n.d., <http://www.middlesexcanal.org/docs/rumford.htm> (March 3, 2008).
4. Robert Price, *Johnny Appleseed: Man and Myth* (Bloomington, Ind.: Indiana University Press, 1954), p. 13.
5. Kathleen Pyle, "Legacy of an Apple Seed," *American Forests*, Spring 1999, p. 21.

CHAPTER 3
The Spirit of Individualism

1. Marji Hazen, "Johnny Appleseed," *Ashland County Chapter of the Ohio Genealogical Society*, n.d., <http://ashlandohiogenealogy.org/johnnyappleseed.html> (March 8, 2008).
2. Robert Price, *Johnny Appleseed: Man and Myth* (Bloomington, Ind.: Indiana University Press, 1954), p. 23.
3. Jeff Meyer, "A Hero for the Ages," *American Forests*, Winter 2003, p. 51.

4. Ibid.
5. Charles Elliot, "The Core of Johnny Appleseed," *Horticulture*, November/December, 1999, p. 24.
6. Tim Hensley, "Apples of Your Eye," *Smithsonian*, November 2002, p. 111.
7. Ibid., p. 112.
8. Meyer, p. 51.
9. Price, p. 29.
10. Frank B. McAllister, "Johnny Appleseed," *Vermont Weather-vine*, Fall 1997, <http://www.ruralvermont.com/vermontweather vane/issues/fall/97009/appleseed.html> (March 3, 2008).
11. Price, p. 30.
12. "John Henry," *Morgantown Dominion-Post*, February 1, 1976, <http://www.wvculture.org/history/africanamericans/henry john02.html> (March 3, 2008).
13. "John Henry," *National Public Radio*, September 2, 2002, <http:www.npr.org/programs/morning/features/patc/john henry/index.html> (March 3, 2008).
14. Carlene Hempel, "The Man—Facts, Fiction and Themes," *John Henry, the Steel Driving Man*, December 1998, <http://www.ibiblio.org/john_henry/analysis.html> (March 3, 2008).

CHAPTER 4
The Moveable Nursery

1. Rosella Rice, *Johnny Appleseed* (Mansfield, Ohio: Little Journeys Bookshop, 2001), p. 2.
2. Robert Price, *Johnny Appleseed: Man and Myth* (Bloomington, Ind.: Indiana University Press, 1954), pp. 167–168.
3. Rice, p. 2.
4. Edward Hoagland, "Johnny Appleseed," in *A Sense of History: The Best Writing from the Pages of American Heritage* (New York: American Heritage Press, 1985), p. 196.
5. Tim Hensley, "Apples of Your Eye," *Smithsonian*, November 2002, p. 112.
6. Price, p. 49.
7. Rickie Longfellow, "Zane's Trace," *Federal Highway Administration*, n.d., <http://www.fhwa.dot.gov/infrastructure/back 0803.htm> (March 8, 2008).
8. Hoagland, in *A Sense of History*, p. 196.
9. Ibid.

10. Price, p. 65.
11. Frank B. McAllister, "Johnny Appleseed," *Vermont Weather-vine*, Fall 1997, <http://www.ruralvermont.com/vermontweather vane/issues/fall/97009/appleseed.html> (March 3, 2008).
12. Ophia D. Smith, "The Story of Johnny Appleseed," in William Ellery Jones, ed., *Johnny Appleseed, A Voice in the Wilderness* (West Chester, Pa.: Chrysalis Books, 2000), p. 73.
13. Ibid.
14. Price, p. 168.
15. William Ellery Jones, "New Information about an Old Friend," in William Ellery Jones, ed., *Johnny Appleseed, A Voice in the Wilderness* (West Chester, Pa.: Chrysalis Books, 2000), p. 101.

CHAPTER 5
The War of 1812

1. Rosella Rice, *Johnny Appleseed* (Mansfield, Ohio: Little Journeys Bookshop, 2001), p. 10.
2. Frank B. McAllister, "Johnny Appleseed," *Vermont Weather-vine*, Fall 1997, <http://www.ruralvermont.com/vermontweather vane/issues/fall/97009/appleseed.html> (March 3, 2008).
3. "Konieschquanoheel," *Ohio History Central*, Ohio Historical Society, 2008, <http://www.ohiohistorycentral.org/entry.php? rec=98> (March 18, 2008).
4. Ibid.
5. Carl Benn, *The War of 1812* (New York: Routledge (USA), 2003), p. 16.
6. Ibid., p. 26.
7. Ibid., p. 30.
8. Ibid., p. 34.
9. A.J. Baughman, "History of Richland County," The USGen Web Project, n.d., <http://www.rootsweb.com/~ohrichla/ Hist-Mansfield1903.htm> (March 18, 2008).
10. Robert Price, *Johnny Appleseed: Man and Myth* (Bloomington, Ind.: Indiana University Press, 1954), p. 88.
11. Ibid., p. 90.
12. "The Copus Massacre," *Ashland County Historical Society*, 2006–2008, <http://ashlandhistory.org/index.php?section= history&content=copus_massacre> (March 18, 2008).
13. Benn, p. 46.

CHAPTER 6
Business and Religion

1. Frank B. McAllister, "Johnny Appleseed," *Vermont Weather-vine*, Fall 1997, <http://www.ruralvermont.com/vermont weathervane/issues/fall/97009/appleseed.html> (March 3, 2008).
2. Robert Price, *Johnny Appleseed: Man and Myth* (Bloomington, Ind.: Indiana University Press, 1954), p. 110.
3. Edward Hoagland, "Johnny Applesccd," in *A Sense of History: The Best Writing from the Pages of American Heritage* (New York: American Heritage Press, 1985), p. 189.
4. Ophia D. Smith, "The Story of Johnny Appleseed," in William Ellery Jones, ed., *Johnny Appleseed, A Voice in the Wilderness* (West Chester, Pa.: Chrysalis Books, 2000), p. 79.
5. Rosella Rice, *Johnny Appleseed* (Mansfield, Ohio: Little Journeys Bookshop, 2001), p. 4.
6. Price, p. 114.
7. Hoagland, in *A Sense of History*, pp. 186–187.
8. Ibid., p. 190.
9. Christine Leigh Heyrman, "The First Great Awakening," *Divining America, Religion in American History*, The National Humanities Center, January 2008, <http://national humanitiescenter.org/tserve/eighteen/ekeyinfo/grawaken .htm> (March 23, 2008).
10. Donald Scott, "Evangelicalism, Revivalism, and the Second Great Awakening," *The 19th Century*, The National Humanities Center, 2000, <http://nationalhumanitiescenter .org/tserve/nineteen/nkeyinfo/nevanrev.htm> (March 23, 2008).
11. John W. Stockwell, "The Religion of Johnny Appleseed," in William Ellery Jones, ed., *Johnny Appleseed: A Voice in the Wilderness*, pp. 61–62.
12. William E. Leuchtenburg, "John Chapman (Johnny Appleseed)," in Susan Ware, ed., *Forgotten Heroes* (New York: Free Press, 1998), p. 13.
13. Smith, in *Johnny Appleseed, A Voice in the Wilderness*, p. 73.
14. Price, p. 125.
15. Ibid., p. 128.
16. Jeff Meyer, "A Hero for the Ages," *American Forests*, Winter 2003, p. 51.
17. Leuchtenburg, in *Forgotten Heroes*, p. 13.

18. Hoagland, in *A Sense of History*, p. 192.
19. William Ellery Jones, "New Information about an Old Friend," in William Ellery Jones, ed., *Johnny Appleseed: A Voice in the Wilderness*, pp. 110–111.
20. Price, p. 131.

CHAPTER 7
Chapman Transforms the West

1. Robert Price, *Johnny Appleseed: Man and Myth* (Bloomington, Ind.: Indiana University Press, 1954), pp. 149–150.
2. Ibid., p. 175.
3. Ibid., p. 189.
4. Ibid., pp. 187–188.
5. Ibid., p. 210.
6. Rosella Rice, *Johnny Appleseed* (Mansfield, Ohio: Little Journeys Bookshop, 2001), p. 11.
7. Edward Hoagland, "Johnny Appleseed," in *A Sense of History: The Best Writing from the Pages of American Heritage* (New York: American Heritage Press, 1985), p. 198.
8. William E. Leuchtenburg, "John Chapman (Johnny Appleseed)," in Susan Ware, ed., *Forgotten Heroes* (New York: Free Press, 1998), p. 15.

CHAPTER 8
The Legacy of Johnny Appleseed

1. Robert Price, *Johnny Appleseed: Man and Myth* (Bloomington, Ind.: Indiana University Press, 1954), p. 251.
2. William E. Leuchtenburg, "John Chapman (Johnny Appleseed)," in Susan Ware, ed., *Forgotten Heroes* (New York: Free Press, 1998), p. 16.
3. Price., p. 251.
4. W. D. Haley, "Johnny Appleseed: A Pioneer Hero," *Harper's New Monthly Magazine*, November 1871, <http://mason.gmu.edu/~drwillia/apple/ja8sm.html> (February 27, 2008).
5. Robert Price, "Johnny Appleseed in American Folklore and Literature," in William Ellery Jones, ed., *Johnny Appleseed, A Voice in the Wilderness* (West Chester, Pa.: Chrysalis Books, 2000), p. 32.
6. Price, p. 260.
7. Florence Murdoch, "The Arts Salute Johnny Appleseed," in Jones, *Johnny Appleseed: A Voice in the Wilderness*, p. 50.

8. Ibid., p. 34.

9. Price., p. 224.

10. Ibid., p. 50.

11. Edward Hoagland, "Johnny Appleseed," in *A Sense of History: The Best Writing from the Pages of American Heritage* (New York: American Heritage Press, 1985), p. 191.

12. Kathleen Pyle, "Legacy of An Apple Seed," *American Forests,* Spring 1999, p. 21.

13. Charles Elliot, "The Core of Johnny Appleseed," *Horticulture,* November/December, 1999, p. 25.

GLOSSARY

apple butter—A soft spread made from mashing and churning apples.

apple vinegar—A preservative made with apple juice, used to pickle vegetables.

blockhouse—A tall, wooden structure built to preserve a settlement.

carpels—Sections of an apple containing seeds.

grafting—Combining one plant with another to create a superior planting.

Great Awakening—The religious revival in the United States in the eighteenth and nineteenth centuries.

nursery—A place where trees and plants are grown for sale to customers.

quarter section—A piece of square property measuring 160 acres.

seedling—A small, young tree.

Swedenborgian—A religious group that arose during the nineteenth century.

Transcendentalism—A spiritual movement that arose in New England during the nineteenth century.

FURTHER READING

Holub, Joan. *Who Was Johnny Appleseed?* New York: Grosset and Dunlop, 2005.

Moses, Will. *Johnny Appleseed: The Story of a Legend.* New York: Puffin Books, 2004.

Schaefer, Lola. *Johnny Appleseed.* Mankato, Minn.: Pebble Books, 2003.

Yolen, Jane. *Johnny Appleseed.* New York: HarperCollins Publishers, 2008.

Zarzycki, Daryl Davis. *Johnny Appleseed.* Hockessin, Del.: Mitchell Lane Publishers, 2007.

INTERNET ADDRESSES

Johnny Appleseed Educational Center and Museum,
National Apple Museum
**<http://www.nationalapplemuseum.com/
johnny.html>**

Johnny Appleseed Festival
**<http://www.johnnyappleseedfest.com/index
.html>**

Johnny Appleseed Heritage Center, Inc.
<http://www.jahci.org/project.html>

INDEX